No Such Thing As
Luck

A Biblical Perspective
Charlie P. Johnston Jr.

No Such Thing As
Luck

A Biblical Perspective

No Such Thing As Luck
A Biblical Perspective

The Scriptures used throughout this book are quoted from the *Authorized* or *King James Version* unless otherwise noted. All explanatory insertions within a Scripture verse are enclosed in square brackets. All non-English words are printed with English letters and italicized.

Published by: **Johnston Publications**
P.O. Box 13
Greenwood, FL 32443
(850)592-8769
www.johnstonpublications.com

ISBN#0-9743339-1-3
Library of Congress Catalogue Card Number : 2004113271
Published 2005
Printed in the United States of America

Dedication

To my brothers and sisters born-again of God's spirit, who are looking forward with anticipation to the blessed hope and return of Jesus Christ, our Living Lord and Savior. What a day that will be!

Contents

Chapter One
Introducing Luck's Controversy................................15
Chapter Two
The Origin of "Luck Theology".......................................41
Chapter Three
"Luck Theology" in the Promised Land of Canaan....55
Chapter Four
"Luck Theology" in Greece and Rome.........................73
Chapter Five
'Fickled' Fate...93
Chapter Six
Destiny's Deception...119
Chapter Seven
A Little About A Lot..139
Chapter Eight
Fortune's Fallacy...157
Chapter Nine
Chances Are? There are No Chances Are!................181
Chapter Ten
No Chance for Chance!..207
Chapter Eleven
The Myth of Mythology..229
Chapter Twelve
Luck's Real Meaning...265
Scriptural Index...294

PREFACE

This book is written to those who are already born again of God's spirit and those who will become so. I am the first to realize that this book will have little appeal to those who fit neither of these two categories. However, anyone might find it of interest to understand the origin and development of **luck**'s meaning. When the supposed action of **luck** or **chance** is removed as a possibility for the cause of any event, we are then in a far better position to understand truth. This book seeks to remove the **luck** factor from our thinking and believing.

Deceiving beliefs and teachings about **luck, fate, destiny, lot, fortune,** and **chance** abound worldwide. Society, as a whole, embraces these ideas. The Christian community of believers is bombarded constantly by all of these wayward notions. The purpose of this work is to alert and enlighten God's people regarding the idolatrous nature and meaning of these popular belief systems. After reading this book, no one need fall prey to these cleverly devised concepts with their crafty meanings.

Either a man is willing to show meekness toward the Word of God or he is hard-hearted. This book is addressed to the meek of heart; those who rejoice in the Truth. The non-denominational, non-sectarian approach of this work should make it a helpful and relevant source of information and enlightenment to Christian believers worldwide.

******

This book is written with the resolve that God's Word can be trusted over and above any man's word. The author also believes the Bible [God's Word] is the only reliable foundation for life and living and every diligent, honest searching of the Bible will produce meaningful answers. Consequently, this book should appeal to Christian believers who love the Bible and its contents. This work is offered to the serious-hearted believer who is willing to investigate its contents and be challenged to change their thinking when it is necessary.

******

The choice to utilize the *1968 College Edition of Webster's New World Dictionary* as a primary source is based upon its widespread availability and its ease of readability.

ACKNOWLEDGMENTS

Diamond Lee Ford, Wayne Clapp, Ann Musgroves, Gary and Becky Sheirer, and my daughter Elizabeth, all made this a better book by their helpful input and diligent critiquing. Their giving is a sweet smelling savor. My son Daniel helped with the cover design and illustrations. He is fourteen and already a diligent, discipled young man who loves God's Word.

My loving wife Carol stood by my side and supported my every endeavor with this book. She has done that faithfully with my every undertaking. She researched, typed and retyped over and over again, corrected, clarified, simplified and improved the text of this book. She did all this with a joyful, giving heart. What a wife! What a friend and helper! - My bride of over twenty-five years.

My sons Chuck, Dean, Tim, and Chris would have helped, had they been asked, but the geography of half a continent was inconvenient for us. My mother Ollie Mae was delighted to see the completion of this book.

Neither give heed to fables [myths] and endless genealogies, which minister questions, rather than godly edifying which is in faith: so do.

1 Timothy 1:4

CHAPTER ONE

Introducing Luck's Controversy

What **luck** is, where it came from, and its true meaning, are going to become fully evident as we move through the pages of this book. **Luck** is a much-used word in our modern-day vocabulary. We hear this word over and over again. Good **luck** and bad **luck** are concepts we have known about from our youth. References to **luck**, being the direct cause behind this-and-that event, are as commonplace to us as the daily rising of the sun.

We have grown fully accustomed to hearing **luck** used by people in every segment of our society. We have heard it spoken by well-meaning friends and acquaintances. We have heard it spoken regularly by the average person on the street, but its use is certainly not limited to the "average person."

No Such Thing As Luck

The word **luck** is also commonly used among teachers and professors, doctors and lawyers, authors and intellectuals, media commentators and journalists.

The use of the word **luck** has become so commonplace and acceptable that people rarely think seriously about its real meaning. The public's ear has become conditioned by having heard it so often. They have been "lulled to sleep" by its repeated use. Hardly anyone challenges this word; nor is there any sense of embarrassment for having uttered it. Start to train your ear and you will hear its insatiable use!

Actually, the credibility of **luck** is just assumed by a large segment of our population. They are not bothered or irritated by its having been used in their presence or in a conversation with them. As a matter-of-fact, the public at large has bought heavily into this word; they have fully accepted its concept. They have breathed it in, so to speak, and made it an acceptable part of their logic, but by speaking it casually, they validate its preposterous meaning. Occasionally, people appear to be clowning around, in lighthearted jest, with their use of this word; but more often than not, they seriously believe in **luck** with a truthful conviction. They are convinced that **luck** is real.

Sadly, the **luck** terminology we hear in our everyday lives is more than just idle talk. The concept of **luck** is embraced as truth by countless millions. They use it as if it were a truthful explanation for both catastrophic and favorable happenings. If their house burnt down, without any hesitation, they would explain that it was bad **luck**. If they won the lottery, they would attribute good **luck** as the cause. For some, it is an acceptable explanation of why bad things happen to good people, and of course, why good things happen to those who do not deserve it.

⌘⌘⌘⌘

The varying context in which **luck** is used is almost unbelievable. Its use is extensive and far-reaching. It is used in figures of speech, expressions of belief, common sayings, and as we will see, in many other ways. In the next few pages we are going to highlight some of the popular ways in which **luck** is used. We are already familiar with many of these expressions and beliefs about **luck**. My guess is, you are accustomed to hearing most of them regularly. How often do you hear these common phrases and sayings?

Tough Luck	Best of Luck	Hard Luck
Good Luck	Out of Luck	Pure Luck
Blind Luck	Plain Luck	Push One's Luck
Beginner's Luck	Lady Luck	Wish Me Luck
Lucky	Worse Luck	Luck Upon
Bad Luck	Luck Into It	Lucky Dog

Notice how many different descriptive kinds of **luck** are listed above. You may know of others. I guess "rotten" **luck** is supposed to fit in at the bottom of the barrel, and with "pot" **luck,** you might get anything.

No Such Thing As Luck

Here are a few examples of how **luck** is regularly used as a figure of speech, metaphorically. The vast majority of us will be familiar with these sayings and what they mean.

<u>Saying</u>	<u>Meaning</u>
Better luck next time	an expression of encouragement
As luck would have it	beyond personal control
Try one's luck	to do something without being sure of the outcome
You can never know your luck	you can not be sure your luck will not change
Down on one's luck	hard circumstances
A little luck never hurts	added advantage
Devil's own luck	uncanny good luck
The luck of the draw	an expression of resignation to chance
Push your luck	go too far in an effort or activity
Just my luck	typical occurrence
Happy-go-lucky	easygoing - trusting in luck [1]

These expressive figures of speech are not designed to be harmless, innocent sayings. Rather, they are designed to have an impact upon our thinking and believing. They are loaded with intent and purpose, and they are designed to teach, to instruct, and to motivate us.

The popularity of **luck** is vividly expressed in song titles and musical lyrics. *The Green Book of Songs by Subject* lists over fifty popular song titles about **luck**. [2] Here are just a few titles with which you may be familiar:

Luck Be a Lady Tonight
A Good Run of Bad Luck
I Feel Lucky Today
Luckie One
Some Guys Have All the Luck

Almost any category of contemporary, popular music will include lyrics about **luck**. Some examples follow:

From the musical, *My Fair Lady* – "with a little bit of luck."

From the television show, *Hee Haw* – "if it weren't for bad luck I'd have no luck at all."

From the popular hit song, *God Bless the USA*– "thank my lucky stars."

From *People Who Need People* - "are the luckiest people in the world."

From *Asleep at the Wheel* - "that lucky old sun."

19

No Such Thing As Luck

References to **luck** seem to be particularly popular with songwriters of country music. Many of them like to utilize it as a "catch all" explanation. They use it repeatedly in their musical lyrics. They use it to explain practically every other misunderstood cause under the sun. Try humming some of these:

I Always Get Lucky with You

Just My Luck

I'm Just a Lucky So and So

Hard Luck Woman

Just Lucky I Guess

Running Out of Luck

Sometimes I Get Lucky and Forget

Luck in Love

Some Guys Have All the Luck

You Got Lucky

If I Were a Gambler I Might Have Better Luck

Hard Luck Stories

Till Good Luck Comes My Way

With a Little Luck

Twinkle Twinkle Lucky Star

Mr. Lucky

Books about **luck** abound. The web site *Amazon.com* recently had a listing of over seven hundred books dealing with the subject, **luck**. Do you need "how-to-books" on this subject? Try these:

How to Make Luck

Luck Doesn't Happen By Chance

Make Your Own Luck

Seeds of Luck

Raise Your Luck High

Create Your Own Good Luck

About Your Luck

Dream Power: Improve Your Luck

Luck Builders

Luck is Where You Find It

How to Control Fate, Luck, Chaos, and Carma

The Fortune Telling Book: (Omens of Love and Luck)

By and large, books that are written about **luck** support the concept. Those that denounce the idea are very few and far between.

References to **luck** abound in literature of all kinds: history, fiction, even science and religion. Evidently, there is no sense of embarrassment to journalists for having used this word in printed publications. As you can easily discover by reading your local newspaper, the word **luck** appears regularly, even daily, and often in several articles. It might not be possible to print the sports section of our newspapers without the use of it. Take a look for yourself; the word **luck**

No Such Thing As Luck

will pop out at you in this section of your newspaper right away. For example, in the sports section of our local paper the AP football writer, David Goldberg, started his football article: "In the modern NFL, the salary cap makes depth a matter of chance and luck." [3]

By the way, have you seen any good movies lately? The recent movies, *Lucky Girl, Luckie Me, Lucky Lady, Lucky Seven, Luckie Numbers* and *Pure Luck* may not fit into the category of good movies, nevertheless, **luck** is one of their central themes.

⌘⌘⌘⌘

Advertisers love to use the **luck** word. McDonalds Corporation's 2003-Dollar Menu ad started off with the catchy little rhyme – "Got a Buck? You're in Luck!" The Coca-Cola Corporation followed that same year with their ad campaign that began, "Hey, want to get lucky? The odds are in your favor!" Recently, in our Sunday paper's insert, a California business advertised their fourteen-inch "Lucky Fairy" doll. For just two payments of $12.49 and $5.96 shipping, this supposed magical leprechaun treasure could be yours. (No thanks!)

Proverbs and folk sayings about **luck** abound in the hundreds. Here are just a few to consider:

- Lucky men need no counsel
- Better to be born lucky than rich
- Lucky indeed is he who suffers no ill for one day
- Good luck reaches farther than long arms
- Good luck is easier to win than to retain
- If unlucky today, it will not be always so
- Lucky at cards, unlucky in love

Here are a few common beliefs about **luck**. Maybe you have heard about, or even practiced, some of these:

- Knock on wood to take the bad luck off a brag.
- Try everything three times – the third time for luck.
- Get up and walk around your chair to change your luck at cards.
- Spit on your fishhook for luck, to make fish bite.
- Eat black-eyed peas on New Year's Day for good financial luck all year long. (Pork and sauerkraut in some circles)
- A bride wears something old, something new, something borrowed, and something blue, to bring good luck.
- Kiss a newborn baby for good-luck.
- If a ladybug lights on you, you will have good luck.
- Tossing a coin into a fountain brings good luck.

No Such Thing As Luck

References to **luck** are sometimes made in thoughtlessness. But, this is only true because, somewhere along the way, a conscious decision was made to adopt the validity of **luck's** concept. Then, by using it again and again, a habit was formed. The choice to use this word usually reflects the believing stance, or position, of the user. They have chosen to use it because they have embraced its validity. For them, **luck** has become a valid explanation and expression of their reasoning.

While at the library working on this book, an acquaintance stopped at my table to say, "Hello." Our conversation centered on my writing to expose the fallacy of **luck**. When we finished our chat, my acquaintance walked away uttering these parting words, "Good **luck** on your book." I could not believe my ears, but there it was, right in my face. To me this was a prime example of the seemingly innocent habit of wishing someone good **luck**. Thanks, but no thanks! The choice of almost any other parting words would have been more encouraging. By the way, this was not an isolated incident. Similar conversations with others produced about the same result. People often have difficulty jarring themselves free of **luck** logic.

⌘⌘⌘⌘

The term, "good **luck**," is the standard popular pronouncement on almost any activity where a good outcome is desired or hoped for. Its use is like a prayer, beseeching the force of **luck** for a blessing. We hear it daily:

- Undertaking a difficult task – good luck!
- Looking for a job – good luck!
- Taking a test today – students, good luck!
- If luck smiles on us — the weather will be good for our picnic today.
- If we are lucky – we might catch fish today.
- If "Lady Luck" is with me - I will win the lottery.

Good examples of this common pronouncement can be heard in numerous contexts; for example, the television game show, *Jeopardy*. We might all fall off our chairs if Alex Trebek, *Jeopardy*'s host, failed to speak forth his wishful little prayer of "good **luck**" to his contestants as they start the game. In the sporting event of football, the game starts off with a coin toss, and then, inevitably, the referee offers what is essentially his prayer of blessing: "good **luck**, and may the best team win."

Conversely, most any event with a disastrous or an undesirable outcome is explained by attributing it to "bad **luck**":

- A slippery fall in the tub – bad luck!
- Loss of your wallet – bad luck!
- Lost your tennis match today – bad luck!
- My career is faltering – I'm just having bad luck!
- Rained on our picnic today – bad luck!
- Home burnt down – really bad luck!

The term **luck** is often used to explain the unusual, the odd, and the seemingly supernatural. Participants in sporting contests attach descriptive terms to **luck** constantly. Comments like: "that was a lucky shot, a lucky punch, or a lucky throw" are often heard. Sports commentators are perhaps the biggest offenders. They attribute almost any outstanding or unusual occurrence to some kind of **luck**. Utterances such as: "that catch was pure **luck**," or "that race car driver is pushing his **luck**," or "he's down on his **luck**," are not unusual to hear.

Luck is actively summoned. People actually pursue its blessing. In gambling activities, Lady Luck is the "big star." Vast numbers of those who gamble believe she holds the power to make them winners, and they summon her help. Gamblers frequently carry a rabbit's foot with them, or a special shaped (**lucky**) stone or other superstitious article they believe will bring "Lady Luck" to their side. (Later we will discover how **luck** came to be called a lady.)

Gamblers are not the only superstitious people who pray to **luck**. A large segment of our population believe rituals and magical charms can summon good **luck**. These are the people who wear **lucky** clothes or a **lucky** cap. They choose to sit in their same **lucky** chair. They perform little **lucky** rituals before the start of events in which they participate. People of this persuasion wear charm bracelets and other special objects such as talismans, which they believe have magical powers and will help to procure them **luck**'s blessing.

Individuals not only believe good **luck** can be summoned, they also believe bad **luck** can be warded off. People with this conviction wear amulets. Amulets are used to ward off and protect against evil. Those who believe bad **luck** can be warded off avoid the path of black cats; they avoid walking under ladders; they toss spilt salt over their left shoulder. They would never open an umbrella in the house. They believe that by wearing objects which possess magical powers, their lives are protected from ill **fortune** or bad **luck**.

> There is a tremendous demand, year in and year out, for the Virginia Fairy Crosses, or lucky stones, for watch charms or lockets to be worn as amulets against witchcraft, to prevent disease, or to avert misfortune generally. [4]

In passing, it needs to be pointed out, talismans (to bring good **luck**) and amulets (to ward off bad **luck**) are not only worn but are often displayed. A case in point is the rear-view mirrors of automobiles. Just take a look and you will see all kinds of objects: beads, medallions, Saint Christophers, tassels, dice, rings. This activity is not based upon an innocent, meaningless, cultural practice. This practice is based upon a belief in the effectiveness of these objects to secure the blessing of good **luck**, and to ward off bad **luck**, while people are traveling.

The Irish have built a sizeable part of their culture around claiming protection against bad **luck**. They are quick to lay the blame upon it when they believe it strikes their lives. Everyone has heard about "the **luck** of the Irish." Their persuasions about leprechauns and shamrocks, and a host of other superstitious beliefs, are as current today as in earlier years. The movie, *The Luck of the Irish*, features a story of a teenager who must battle for a gold charm to keep his family from being controlled by an evil leprechaun.

⌘⌘⌘⌘

No Such Thing As Luck

The ridiculous absurdity of **luck**'s use goes on and on. Before we end our survey, take a look at the following hard-to-believe applications of this word in the marketplace:

The *Hi Continental Corporation* cans and distributes a product they call *Double Luck* green beans.

You can find the *Lucky Spa* massage parlor off Highway 75 near Tifton, Georgia, and the *Luckie 13 Truck Stop* on Interstate 10, near DeFuniak Springs, Florida.

You can order a *Lucky Angel Bingo Pin* from current gift catalogues.

Looking for toilettes? *Lucky You* fragrance sets are available from a firm by the name of *Lucky You*.

Need a mantel piece? Lenox markets a *Touch of Luck* elephant sculpture – it is 3½" H x 3" W.

The next trip to the grocery store remember to buy *Lucky Charms* cereal.

Lucky Craft Incorporated announced their new *Symbol VIB* fish lure in February of 2003.

Be advised – a Florida based company, *"B" Lucky Auto Sales*, has just the car they think you need!

I almost forgot, *Harriet Carter's* gift catalogue sells a black, 100% cotton tee-shirt with the following message printed in white and gold – *At My Age "Getting Lucky" Is Finding My Car In The Parking Lot.*

Categories and context involving the use of **luck** are unbelievably numerous. Its use is prolific, but we have seen enough. Now it is time for us to get more serious about our use of this word.

⌘ ⌘ ⌘ ⌘

Immediately, we can consider two aspects about **luck**. We use the term "good **luck**", but we also use the term "bad **luck**." Obviously, this makes the concept confusing and complicated. These two common concepts of **luck** are contrary to one another; it is not all-good, nor is it all-evil. These expressions are actually antithetical; they are set against each other. Essentially, **luck** is viewed as a fickle, flip-flop, haphazard force of action, working good and evil upon and around our lives. If this is true, all of us are in serious trouble!

We need to understand all that we can about **luck's** fundamental concept and its true meaning. This is indeed the right time to start asking some realistic questions about our use of this word. Here are a few forthright questions that might help us to think more soundly about this subject:

♦ Is the force acting behind "good **luck**" the same as the force that acts behind "bad **luck**" or do we have two separate forces acting independently?

♦ How and why does **luck** choose whom it will bless or curse?

No Such Thing As Luck

- ◆ Why is bad **luck** visited upon the seemingly innocent?

- ◆ What is **luck** in its essence — is it a living entity?

- ◆ How did **luck** get started and from where did it come?

- ◆ Just how powerful are these supposed forces of good and bad **luck** — are they ultimate powers?

- ◆ Is God the bestower of **luck**?

- ◆ Does **luck** exist independent of God?

- ◆ Is the power of **luck** greater than God?

- ◆ Does **luck** control our lives, leaving us no recourse?

- ◆ Can **luck** make us successful, wealthy superstars?

- ◆ Can **luck** walk into our lives at its will to wreck us, crush us, take from us, and ultimately defeat us?

These questions deserve honest and forthright answers. We truly must have relevant and accurate explanations for all these questions. We need to know where and how the concept of **luck** got its start, but we also need to understand both why and how its teachings flourish today! The enlightenment of biblical understanding is going to provide the meaningful answers we are seeking.

As we will soon see, the weight and enlightenment of God's Word deals with our subject authoritatively. By using God's Word and the testimony of history, we will now begin to focus upon and answer these serious questions. Our discussion of these important questions is designed to expose the pathetic claims and teachings that surround the subject of **luck**. People who desire an understanding in this category are going to have the opportunity to confront **luck** for what it truly is.

⌘⌘⌘⌘

Maybe you have never seriously looked into the real meaning of what **luck** is all about and what it implies. As we are about to see firsthand, a careful examination of **luck's** teachings and philosophies are disturbing. By probing the various aspects of what is taught about **luck** (its doctrine) we are going to uncover strange, uncanny, and even bizarre reasoning. The boastful teachings of those who embrace **luck's** doctrine abound worldwide. Their sassy, outrageous claims and teachings need a long overdue truthful examination.

No Such Thing As Luck

Listen carefully to their suspicious teachings, and to their obstinate, boastful claims. Their outlandish claims about good **luck** say:

♦ Find a four leaf clover and **luck** will bless you.

♦ Carry a rabbit's foot in your pocket and **luck** will be there for you.

♦ Wear your **lucky** shirt today and you will win the game.

♦ Just cross you fingers and hold them there and **luck** will bless you eventually.

♦ Change your **luck** at cards by drawing a bridge under your score.

♦ Toss a few coins into a fountain and that will bring **luck** to your side.

♦ Stay with your **lucky** numbers and they will help you win the lottery.

♦ Nail a horseshoe to the top of your door and that will attract good **luck** to your life.

♦ Be sure to thank your **lucky** stars because they are out there and they are going to help bring good upon your life.

Conversely, the disciples of bad **luck** have called out just as boisterously with their threats and intimidation. They say:

- Walk under that ladder and you are in for bad **luck**.

- The number 13 is mystical and evil so don't use it.

- If you spill that salt, you are in trouble.

- Avoid this and avoid that or bad **luck** will rain hurt upon you.

- Friday the 13th is, of course, bad **luck**'s day to curse and work havoc.

We have some potentially devastating problems here. If we have adopted the concept of **luck** and are using the terminology, surely that makes us subject to the ups and downs of life. If it is good **luck** we long to have, then we must wait for it to come to us. If it is bad **luck** we fear, then we must guard against the disastrous outcome looming just ahead. Our beliefs about **luck** push us around. **Luck** enters into our life, at its will, to control our good or to cast evil upon us. Where does this leave us? Who wants to be controlled and pushed around? No one!

A confession of dependence upon "good **luck**" diminishes the personal responsibility and work required to bring a thing to pass. It leaves us standing on the sidelines waiting for **luck** to bring good upon our lives. The negative we have confessed is, "My personal work and accomplishments are not great enough, not sufficient, to get the job done."

Again, where does confessing **luck** leave us? It takes away our freedom to control what is happening in our lives. We become helpless and powerless. By embracing the doctrine of **luck**, we have shifted our personal responsibility to something outside of our control. We have become docile, submissive, used and controlled. We have yielded to a supposed force of happenstance that chooses to bless us, or to condemn us at its will and fancy.

No one should ever be duped into crippling promises about **luck**. As we are going to see, all of **luck's** promises add up to nothing more than empty, hot air illusions. Lusting after what **luck** promises diminishes the building of character and morality. Waiting around for the fulfillment of **luck's** claims undermines discipline. Teachings about **luck** foster the "free-loader" mentality of getting something for nothing. The boastful doctrinal claims of **luck** also set forth instructions that advocate the use of magic and the practice of meaningless, ridiculous rituals.

⌘⌘⌘⌘

It is important that we start to look behind **luck's** promises of good and its threats of harm. We need to see the underlying motives behind its outrageous claims and intimidating threats and we need to aggressively dissect commonly accepted beliefs that surround **luck**. We also need to thoroughly examine the purposes and the intentions of those who continue to pawn off their vain beliefs for truth.

The fundamental claim of **luck** is power. **Luck** claims the power to bring benefits and to bestow blessings. It claims the ability to protect and to care for us, and claims the ability to supply our needs and wants. It also claims the ability to bring harm upon our lives. All these claims add up to something of great importance, if they are factual. If the assertions made by **luck** are true, we have an exalted god-force operating in and about our lives, and this force is not the God and Father of our Lord, Jesus Christ! This wayward doctrine is exactly what the proponents of **luck** are setting forth. They teach, "The god-force of **luck** is alive and operating in the universe today." However, their teachings are not new.

Throughout history, there have always been those who have stood up and proclaimed **luck**'s truth. They say it is real, that it exists, and it operates either for them or against them. Our generation is no different. People today are still confessing these same beliefs about **luck**. They continue to teach the validity of its power. As we will shortly see, up until this very day, **luck** remains a controversial subject.

⌘⌘⌘⌘

No Such Thing As Luck

Current controversial beliefs about **luck** are not harmless games or innocent jesting, nor do they concern questions of ignorance, as some suppose. The controversy that surrounds **luck** deals with something of vast importance. It is about the reasons and causes behind some of the critical events in our lives. A confession of **luck** ultimately centers on the important question of naming and explaining the forces operating about us, upon us, and ultimately even in us.

Luck claims the power to act and to bring great things to pass. The problem with this is the big claims and promises of **luck** stand in direct opposition to God, the Creator of heaven and earth. What is said and taught about **luck** stands diametrically opposed to what God has to say in His Word.

The controversy here is between those who choose to embrace and elevate the claims and promises of **luck** over the abiding certainty of God and what He has promised to us in His Word. God's promises are openly laid before us in the truth and accuracy of His Word. The testimony of countless thousands throughout the ages of history has been, "God is Faithful to His Matchless Word; What God has promised in His Word, He will do." God's promises to us are, "Yea" and "Amen". His promises are also to every individual, man, woman and child, without partiality. Any individual who becomes persuaded of God and acts upon His Word will absolutely receive the blessings God has promised. The reality of what God has made available to us can be appropriated by belief; our receiving equals our believing.

36

An outstanding example of God's promises in the financial category is found in the Old Testament book of Malachi:

> Bring ye all the tithes into the storehouse, that there may be meat in Mine house, and prove Me now herewith, saith the Lord of hosts, if I will not open you the windows of heaven, and pour you out a blessing, that *there shall* not *be room* enough *to receive it.*
>
> Malachi 3:10

God's Word proclaimed to the Old Testament nation of Israel can be paraphrased this way: "Honor Me with your finances. Place Me, God, first in your hearts. Give to Me the proportion which I ask of you, and as you do so, I will pour out blessings upon your life, so much so, you just will not be able to receive it all. That is My promise to you; that is My claim; just give it a try and you will see it come to pass!"

Whenever Israel honored God's Word in this manner, they always prospered. They literally received what God had promised them. This same promise stands today for any individual who decides to put God to a personal test in the financial category. God makes a claim in His Word and He absolutely delivers to anyone who acts upon His Word. God is always faithful to His Word. He always performs His promises.

No Such Thing As Luck

God says of the man that delights in His Word:

> And he shall be like a tree planted by the rivers of water, that bringeth forth his fruit in his season, his leaf also shall not wither; and whatsoever he doeth shall prosper.
>
> Psalm 1:3

The Apostle Paul boasts of God:

> But my God shall supply all your need according to His riches in glory by Christ Jesus.
>
> Philippians 4:19

The most fundamental knowledge and experience we have of God is that He cares for us. We humans do have needs. We need help which is outside of, and bigger than, our human capacities. We need to prosper and to be in health. We need protection from harm's way. We also need peace of mind, understanding, and guidance. God has both proclaimed and demonstrated what He will do to meet our needs.

The proponents and promoters of **luck** doubt God's Word. They have proclaimed, "**Luck** will supply, **luck** will protect." Consequently, this great controversy which surrounds **luck** is about belief. It centers on what, or whom, we choose to believe. Are we going to embrace God and His Word or will we embrace **luck** and that which is taught about it? The doctrinal claims of **luck** do not please God! Every aspect of **luck** contradicts God's Word. To confess a belief in **luck** is to countermand and deny God's Word. But, to believe God's Word is to toss the fruitless doctrines of **luck** behind us and to move ahead confidently with what God has promised.

38

The following pages of this book are going to unravel the ongoing controversy that has surrounded **luck** throughout the ages. The goal for the chapters that lie ahead is to expose every pertinent aspect of **luck's** attempt to undermine sound thinking and believing. The negative, hurtful influences that emanate from the concept of **luck** are going to come to light. The reader is going to gain an understanding of just how extensively the doctrines of **luck** have permeated both historical and modern-day reasoning. Chapter Two will begin to trace the origin of **luck**.

---

[1] *The Oxford English Dictionary*, Second Edition, Clarendon Press., Oxford, s.v. "luck"

[2] Green, Jeff, *The Green Book of Songs by Subject*, 4th edition, Professional Desk References, Inc., Nashville, TN, pp.357-358

[3] Goldberg, David, "In the Thin NFL, Depth can be a Matter of Luck", *Jackson County Floridan*, 9 Oct. 2001, p. 2B

[4] de Lys, Claudia, *What's so Lucky About a Four-leaf Clover?*, Bell Publishing Co., NY, 1989, pp. 444

Provide for my needs
and keep me safe.

CHAPTER TWO

The Origin of
"Luck Theology"

Before we begin to trace the origin for the concept of **luck**, we need to understand how the concepts of **fate, lot, fortune,** and **chance** fit into our study. Our dictionaries generally use all of these companion terms in defining **luck**. *Webster's New World Dictionary* gives the following definition:

> Luck: The seemingly chance happening of events which affect one; fortune; lot; fate. [1]

The word **destiny** is going to be added to our study because it is an "offspring" to the concept of **fate**. Additionally, the concept of **destiny** is currently so "alive" that it needs to be handled as a pertinent aspect of this study. There are still other words that we will consider later, but for now, we are going to look briefly at the relationship between **luck** and these companion terms.

No Such Thing As Luck

As we will see, all these words are used interchangeably. **Luck** means **chance**; **chance** means **luck**; **luck** means **fortune**; **fortune** means **luck**. And although **destiny** does not appear in the above definition, it is often used to define **fate**. **Fate** is always nearby in any definition of **luck**. **Lot** appears occasionally in defining **luck**. These terms are generally lumped together in **luck**'s definition. They are actually used so interchangeably that it will be necessary to sort out their individual meanings. (In later chapters, we will examine them, one-by-one, with enough depth to establish their real essence.)

The basic concept of **luck** is ancient, but the word itself is relatively modern. It dates back to only about 1300 AD in its English form. (We will deal with its etymology at a later time.) Our contemporary use of **luck** simply conveys the older, established concepts of **fate, destiny, lot, fortune,** and **chance**. Because of this, we must begin to deal with these earlier words before we tackle **luck**.

All five of these terms refer to spiritual powers and attributes. They seek to define and describe metaphysical forces. Generally speaking, those who utilize these words are seeking to describe what they believe to be a spiritual force acting upon human life (usually upon their lives personally). All of these terms refer to the supposed reality and action of a god. Since every one of these five words is a theological concept they will be addressed as such throughout the pages of this book, and rightfully so.

The Origin of "Luck Theology"

♦ The terms "luck theology" and "chance theology," as used in this book, are meant to include each and all of the words: **fate, destiny, lot, fortune,** and **chance.** These two designated terms are going to be used interchangeably in the following narrative to accurately describe all five words collectively. ♦

⌘⌘⌘⌘

Did you ever wonder how talk about **luck** got started, or who first thought about the use of it? The purpose for this chapter is to provide satisfying answers to these questions.

The first thing we must do is to establish the climate that gave birth to the primitive concepts of "luck theology." We can do this accurately by utilizing the biblical record that factually describes the environment from which these concepts emerged. From the book of Romans, we are going to gain an understanding of exactly why and how vain-thinking men began to forsake God. We will see that when they did so, they lost their authority and basis for sound judgment. We are going to see how they literally exchanged the truth of God's Word for a lie, generated by their own arrogant egos. Furthermore, they believed the lie they set forth to be truth.

> For the invisible things of Him [God] from the creation of the world are clearly seen, being understood by the things that are made, *even* His eternal power and Godhead; so that they [all God-rejecting men] are without excuse:

Because that, when they knew God, they glorified Him not as God, neither were thankful; but became vain in their imaginations, and their foolish heart was darkened.

Professing themselves to be wise, they became fools,

And changed the glory of the uncorruptible God into an image made like to corruptible man, and to birds, and fourfooted beasts, and creeping things.

Romans 1:20-23

Here we are taught there is no justification for any individual to be ignorant and unbelieving about God and His reality. Even the invisible things of God are perceivable; they can be understood. There can be, and should be, an absolutely clear understanding about God. Every essential aspect of God that we need to know about (His very nature, His qualities, and His purposes and plans) have been clearly revealed to us. There is not now, and there has never been, any justification or defense for a God-rejecter. God's revelation of Himself is plainly evident. So, the men described to us here in Romans were without excuse. Nevertheless, they denied that God was God. When they should have known God and recognized Him as God they denied Him and His reality. They gave Him no honor, no glory, nor were they thankful to Him. In doing this, they became futile. Their reasoning, and their foolish, reprobate speculations led them to erroneous conclusions.

Speaking with perverted and prideful minds, these God-rejecters became fools who claimed to be wise and knowing. They exchanged God's everlasting revelation of Himself for ridiculous false gods that they both conceived and then constructed by the work of their own hands. God then, gave them over to their free-will choice to desert Him. They had exchanged the truth of God's Word and His creation for something they themselves chose to worship. They chose to worship a lie. They adapted pseudo worship: their man-made gods, their man-made doctrines and philosophies. They set forth their own explanations of the powers operating in and upon the universe.

Here, from this marvelous record in Romans, we have a full explanation of exactly what happened early in human history. Foolish men ascribed the things of God (His power, His prosperity, and His protection) to the false gods of the universe. The false god of **luck** stood near the head of their inept list of deities. Their corrupted minds exchanged the truth of God's Word for lying precepts. Their destructive lies taught, "**Luck** will bless you with prosperity; the god of **luck** will protect your life from harm and disaster, the god of **luck** has greater power than the true God of heaven and earth." What an alarming contrast – the anemic man-made god of **luck** set against God Almighty, the Creator of the world and all that is therein!

It is clearly evident, when these men abandoned God and His Word, they abandoned their true source book and guide for understanding. They proceeded to develop their own private, homespun explanations about almost everything. They vainly attempted to explain the processes and purposes working actively in and behind spiritual matters. They replaced God in their thinking. They replaced His Word with their own limited and confused reasoning. They formulated their own definitions regarding the following:

- Their origin of life

- The influences and powers which were affecting their lives

- Their purpose for existing

- Their standard of good and evil, right and wrong

- Their devotions and affections

It was man's denial of God's plain and evident truth that made way for his ignorance and superstitions to abound. E.W. Bulliger, in his *Companion Bible* accurately describes the process for this corruption of truth.

> All the ancient systems of idolatry, connected with Astrology and Mythology, were.... not original inventions of what was new; but the corruption of what was old, and the perversion of primitive truth.[2]

Men attributed our true God's protection and blessings of prosperity, to their own "man-made" deities. It is here, within this idolatrous context, that we find the emergence of rebellious "luck theology."

The Origin of "Luck Theology"

⌘⌘⌘⌘

Perhaps not many people are familiar with Nimrod, but at this point we are going to consider an important reference to this man from the Bible. The example of his conduct fortifies what we have learned from the Epistle of Romans. Nimrod was the founder of the ancient city of Babylon, located in the early Mesopotamian Civilization.

> And Cush begat Nimrod: he began to be a mighty one in the earth.
>
> He was a mighty hunter before [in defiance of] the Lord; Wherefore it is said, Even as Nimrod the mighty hunter before [in defiance of] the Lord.
>
> Genesis 10:8-9

The name, Nimrod, is used here in the first person plural. Nimrod literally means, "We will rebel." [3] With this in mind, let us look at a first century historian's account of Nimrod. The testimony of Josephus regarding Nimrod carries us back to very early history.

> "Now it was Nimrod who excited them [Noah's ancestry] to such an affront and contempt of God. He was the grandson of

> Ham, the son of Noah, a bold man, and of
> great strength of hand. He persuaded them
> [Noah's ancestry] not to ascribe it [their well
> being] to God, as if it was through his
> [Nimrod's] means they were happy, but to
> believe that it was their own courage which
> procured that happiness. He also gradually
> changed the government into tyranny, seeing
> no other way of turning men from the fear of
> God, but to bring them into a constant
> dependence on his [Nimrod's] power." [4]

From Josephus' prospective, these ancient men were looking within their own capacity for answers concerning their lives, but not to God. This account is graphic regarding outright rebellion against the true God by the men living at that time. Notice how Nimrod began to formulate "man-made" doctrines to explain their condition and welfare. This is a good example of high-minded speculation that led to all kinds of philosophies and theologies, including the "chance theologies" with which we are concerned. The beginning of Nimrod's kingdom was in the land of Shinar (Babylon). His descendants, the early Babylonians, began to devise their own world systems. They redefined events and circumstances that surrounded their lives according to their personal opinions as opposed to God's Word.

Before long, the Babylonians had begun to worship a virtual pantheon of gods in an attempt to explain the spiritual realities and forces affecting their lives. They eventually proclaimed their gods Anu, Ishtar, Ea, and Merodach, to be the powers behind the universe. According to a Babylonian creation myth, the assembly of the gods bestowed upon

Merodach supreme authority and the privilege to determine fates.[5] Merodach ascended in popularity to become the head of all Babylonian deities and was commonly called "Belu" or "Bel," meaning lord. (The biblical usage of this word is generally rendered "Baal.")

When God revealed his plan to destroy Merodach, this so-called, "lord of the gods," He used the Babylonian designation "Bel."[6] The Word of the Lord spoken by Jeremiah, the prophet, described this upcoming event.

> Declare ye among the nations, and publish, and set up a standard; publish, *and* conceal not: say, Babylon is taken, Bel is confounded, Merodach is broken in pieces; her idols are confounded, her images are broken in pieces.
>
> Jeremiah 50:2

And again,

> And I will punish Bel in Babylon, and I will bring forth out of his mouth that which he hath swallowed up: and the nations shall not flow together any more unto him: yea, the wall of Babylon shall fall.
>
> Jeremiah 51:44

Merodach held an astounding influence over the lives of the Babylonians. For centuries they were drawn to his enchanting reputation. They believed he had the power and ability to bring prosperity, as well as destruction. The day was coming when this prideful, false, man-made god would be brought down and removed. However, among the Babylonians before the fifth century B.C., Merodach's powerful reputation flourished. Merodach's ascent to fame dates back to before King Hammurabi, c 1792-1750 B.C.

No Such Thing As Luck

> On the famous diorite monument discovered at Susa, and inscribed with the text of the Babylonian 'code' of laws, Marduk [Merodach] is twice mentioned in the introduction. He had been allotted 'the divine worship of the multitude of the people', and thus before the end of Hammurabi's reign had become the Babylonian national god and patron. [7]

Idolatrous Babylonians handed over the authority and responsibility of governing their personal lives to Merodach and other false gods. Consequently, a big part of life for them centered on determining the will of these gods. What is the will of this god and that god? What is the influence of Merodach in a given matter? How can I determine the will of my god, Bel? That was their $64,000 question. What is the range of Bel's influence upon my life? What must I do to obtain his favor? Uncertainty and doubts about major issues became their way of life.

⌘⌘⌘⌘

What a stark contrast we have here between the closed-off ancient system of idol worship and our personal fellowship with God. The True God, our Heavenly Father, has made His will plain and obvious to everyone. We can count on what God has to say. It is plainly evident! His will is not hidden. What He has to say is also clear and certain. He has had it written in a clear, concise language so that every individual can know and understand His love and care for them. His plans, His purposes, and His designs for all of life are abundantly set forth in His Written Word, the Bible.

There is no guessing about God's Will. His Word is His Will. God is good, so His will for us is good. It will always be for our good. God is never evil. There is just never a time when God will cast or direct evil upon His people. There is never a need to be concerned and fearful about the outcomes of tomorrow. God is on our side. He is always for us and never against us. He surrounds us with His wonderful love and grace. He protects us both day and night.

⌘⌘⌘⌘

Conversely, those Babylonians never knew the will of their false gods. They could only guess. Their disturbing, complex and misguided questions became the seedbed that gave rise to the concepts of **fate, destiny, lot, fortune,** and **chance.** Remember, in their minds, they remained subject to the whims and fancies of their false deities. They were persuaded that the outcomes of events surrounding their lives rested upon their gods. To them, the gods predetermined every important aspect of life. With this mind-set they could only become submissive to the seemingly inevitable.

They believed their lives were predetermined. They became **destined** to the will of Bel. Because they had no recourse, they believed Bel determined their **fate.** The random doling out of Bel's will became their **lot** in life. If Bel's favor was secured, the recipient was **fortunate.** The way Bel performed in a given matter became a **chance** happening.

No Such Thing As Luck

There was really no way to know his will; the options were all his to make. The idol worshipper, in his ignorance, could only speculate; it might go this way or maybe it would go that way. The god's will became a matter referred to as **chance**; it was always "iffy" and unpredictable.

Vain-thinking Babylonians consistently tried to explain the relationship they shared with their false, man-made gods. Their idolatrous ideology begat "luck theology." To confess and embrace concepts like **lot, fate,** and **destiny** required fatalistic belief. But they themselves had chosen and formulated these concepts and then they became enslaved to them. They subjected their lives to their false gods and to the false concepts they said their gods stood for. [In reality, they designed both the false gods and the faulty concepts.] Their idolatrous speculations and theories rapidly became the breeding grounds from which "luck theology" sprang forth. Their worthless reasoning nurtured vicious doomsday fatalistic gods. Their failure to adequately explain spiritual matters and the tangible qualities of cause and effect realities led them to adopt the emptiness of "chance theologies."

⌘ ⌘ ⌘ ⌘

We are going to study the fuller definitions of **fate, destiny, lot, fortune,** and **chance** as they developed through the centuries. However, we have clearly isolated the environment that gave rise to these suspicious words. These words, and the theologies that fostered them are rooted in the idolatry of men like Nimrod and his descendants, the ancient Babylonians.

The Origin of "Luck Theology"

[1] *Webster's New World Dictionary,* World Pub., NY *1968,* s.v. "luck"

[2] Bulliger, E.W., *The Companion Bible,* Zondervan Bible Pub., Grand Rapids, MI, 1974 Appendix 42, p. 36

[3] Ibid., p 15

[4] *The Life and Works of Flavius Josephus,* trans. William Whiston and introd. H. Stebbing, Holt, Rinehart and Winston, NY, p. 39

[5] Caverdish, Richard, *Man, Myth and Magic,* Marshall Caverdish Pub., NY, 1995, pp. 1633-34

[6] Young, Robert, *Analytical Concordance to the Bible,* Wm. B. Eerdmans Publishing Co., Grand Rapids, MI, 1976, p. 86

[7] Caverdish, p. 1633

The Bible names the specific gods of **destiny** and **fortune** to whom the nation of Israel bowed.

CHAPTER THREE

"Luck Theology" in the Promised Land of Canaan

The next development we are going to study is the overwhelming negative influence of Assyrian and Egyptian **luck** gods upon the descendants of Abraham. The Babylonians were not the only people to fabricate "chance theologies." Before 2,000 B.C., their neighbors the Assyrians had developed their own varieties. Eventually, the pagan theologies of these two major empires became so intermingled that it is rather difficult to keep them separated. For the purposes of our study, we are going to keep it simple and refer to the blended varieties they jointly produced. It is significant in history that out of the midst of these idolatrous kingdoms, a man named Abraham responded to the True God's calling.

> Now the Lord had said unto Abram
> [Abraham], Get thee out of thy country, and

> from thy kindred, and from thy father's house,
> unto a land that I will shew thee:
>
> And I will make of thee a great nation, and I
> will bless thee, and make thy name great; and
> thou shalt be a blessing:
>
> Genesis 12:1-2

Abraham grew up among Assyrian idolaters. He knew the popular deities worshipped by the people among whom he lived. His father, Terah, had worshipped pagan idols. In response to God's tremendous calling and His promises, Abraham left Mesopotamia and traveled throughout the region of Canaan. By following the great patriarch Abraham into the Promised Land of Canaan and studying a little about his ancestry we can see first hand how Assyrian "luck theology" hood-winked Israel. References in the Bible name the specific gods and goddesses of **destiny** and **fortune** to whom the nation of Israel bowed. We are going to examine some of these candid records.

It was in Canaan that Jacob, Abraham's grandson, was born. When it was time for Jacob to choose a wife, he traveled from the land of Canaan back to Mesopotamia. There he could take a wife from his father's ancestry. A lively example of Assyrian "luck theology" can be seen by reviewing a record that is related to Jacob's Assyrian wives, Leah and Rachel.

Jacob married Leah and Rachel, daughters of Labon, his uncle. Labon was an Assyrian who practiced idolatry. After his long period of service to Labon (20 years), Jacob sets out for his homeland of Canaan, but with no announcement to Labon of his abrupt departure. Jacob's wife, Rachel, secretly stole-away the household gods [Teraphim] of Labon, her father. Labon hotly pursued Jacob and after catching up to him had this to say:

> It is in the power of my hand to do you hurt but the God of your father spake unto me yesternight, saying, Take thou heed that thou speak not to Jacob either good or bad.

> And now, *though* thou wouldest needs be gone, because thou sore longest after thy father's house, *yet* wherefore has thou stolen my gods?
> Genesis 31:29-30

The God of Jacob was not Labon's god. Labon worshipped pagan Assyrian idols that he thought Jacob had stolen from him. His idolatrous life influenced both of his daughters, Rachel and Leah. Rachel obviously valued the gods of her father, or why would she have stolen them?

We can see Labon's influence on Leah in an earlier record. Leah's handmaid, Zilpah, became Jacob's wife and bore him a son whom Leah named Gad.

> And Zilpah, Leah's maid, bore Jacob a son.

> Then Leah said, Victory and good fortune have come; and she named him Gad [fortune].
> Genesis 30:10 -11 (Amplified Bible)

The name, "Gad," that Leah gave to the son of Zilpah, her handmaid, is actually a reference to the Assyrian god, Baal-Gad (Lord Jupiter, a god of fortune). Leah believed Baal-Gad had shed his good **fortune** upon her with the birth of this son to her handmaid. She thought Baal-Gad was the cause behind the gift of this child. So, her response was to name him after this "god of good **fortune**." To use our modern terminology, "she had been smiled upon by GOOD LUCK!" To Leah's credit, she did give the true God His rightful credit with the birth of her fifth and sixth sons.

⌘⌘⌘⌘

Assyrian religious influence grew to dominate much of the Near East. Their brands of pagan theologies saturated the smaller cultures throughout the region. The same Babylonian and Assyrian "chance theologies" Abraham had left behind soon swallowed up the land of Canaan. Abraham's ancestry was tempted and beguiled over the centuries of their history by numerous Assyrian gods and goddesses. Even in their Egyptian home of Goshen the children of Israel felt the influence of Assyrian power and theology.

> For thus saith the Lord God, My people went down aforetime into Egypt to sojourn there; and the Assyrian oppressed them without cause.
>
> Isaiah 52:4

An Assyrian Pharaoh named Rameses ruled Egypt during a substantial part of the Children of Israel's long Egyptian captivity. [1] A kinship between Assyrian and Egyptian religious belief is easy to detect, especially in the categories related to fate or destiny. We can get a good sense of this kinship by studying how it worked its deleterious influence upon the Israelites during their wilderness wanderings.

God fought for the captive nation of Israel. He worked mighty signs and wonders to bring about their freedom from Egyptian bondage. However, in the face of God's wonderful deliverance they turned to goddess worship quickly after only three short months in the wilderness of Zin. Exposure to the goddess Isis while they were in Egypt helped to entice Israel into idolatrous practices. Isis eventually became the principal goddess of the Egyptians. The name Isis is a Greek word meaning, *who saves or delivers.*

> The Egyptians believed that Isis first taught them agriculture. She is represented in various forms. In one she has the form of a woman, with the horns of a cow, as the cow was sacred to her. [2]

Isis became fully identified with the well-known cow-goddess, Hathor, by the time of the Israelite's exodus from Egypt.

> The most famous cow-goddess was Hathor. She was not only a symbol of fertility but also a sky-goddess, regarded as the Eye of the Sun God, Re; and as the personification of the sky itself. The Egyptians thought of her as a gigantic cow which straddled the earth, her legs marking the four cardinal points. Between her horns she carried the sun's disk; her belly was the sky, her hide and udders were the stars and planets. [3]

No Such Thing As Luck

Barbara Walterson, who authored the above quote, believed Hathor to have been associated directly with the concept of **fate**. According to her, the Egyptians believed their cow-god Hathor had the power to foretell even the **fate** of newborn children.

When Pharaoh called for Moses to go and sacrifice cattle in the land of Egypt, Moses' response was a refusal. He knew the Egyptians considered certain types of cattle sacred and devoted to their goddess, Hathor.

> And Pharaoh called for Moses and for Aaron, and said, Go ye, sacrifice to your God in the land.
>
> And Moses said, It is not meet so to do; for we shall sacrifice the abomination of the Egyptians [the act of sacrificing cattle] to the Lord our God; lo, shall we sacrifice the abomination of the Egyptians [the act of sacrificing cattle] before their eyes, and will they not stone us?
>
> Exodus 8:25-26

The Egyptian Zodiac of Denerah actually used the name Isis when referring to our constellation Taurus, the Bull. [4] The evidence clearly points to this Egyptian goddess Isis [or Hathor as she became known] becoming one of the idols worshipped by the Israelites in the wilderness. The scripture reference below reports Israel's conclusion concerning their deliverance from Egyptian bondage.

"Luck Theology" In The Promised Land Of Canaan

And the Lord said unto Moses, Go, get thee down; for thy people, which thou broughtest out of the land of Egypt, have corrupted *themselves:*

They have turned aside quickly out of the way which I commanded them: they have made them a molten calf, and have worshipped it, and have sacrificed thereunto, and said, These *be* thy gods, O Israel, which have brought thee up out of the land of Egypt.

Exodus 32:7-8

Worship of the golden calf by the Israelites was a turning from glorying in their God - Jehovah, who had delivered them, to glorying in the cow-goddess Hathor. Doubting and deserting God, they attributed their deliverance to her power. They besought her guidance and direction. To her they sacrificed their treasures and their wealth.

The great signs, miracles, and wonders that God Almighty had shown the children of Israel were not enough. They wanted something they could see and feel and handle for a god. So, they gave up God's glory and exchanged it for the empty glory of the phony, **fate** goddess, Hathor, and other associated gods like Moloch.

They made a calf in Horeb, and worshipped the molten image.

Thus they changed their glory into the similitude of an ox that eateth grass.

Psalms 106:19-20

61

No Such Thing As Luck

This golden calf or ox was a smaller symbol of something much larger. What this ox symbolized was directly overhead and in plain view. They could see it! They began to worship the star configuration of Taurus, the Bull. They observed and divined Saturn's movement through this constellation. This became Israel's method for reading and determining what they believed was the will of the Egyptian god Hathor and the Ammonite god Moloch. They believed these gods were going to determine their **destiny**!

> He [God] "gave them [Israel] up to serve the host of heaven". The worship of the golden calf was star worship; it was the solar bull, the constellation Taurus, in which the sun was at the time of the spring equinox. [5]

⌘⌘⌘⌘

The children of Israel quickly turned to Moloch worship because he was one of the dominant idols of the region through which they wandered for forty years. They did not sit down and write out "the order of worship" for this star-king god. They did not make him up on the spot; they adopted him. They turned to him, adopting the established theology that had already been developed around this vicious star-planet god by Near Eastern Ammonites. They worshipped this star-god of **destiny** all along, from the time of their wilderness wandering until the time of their removal from the Promised Land of Canaan. Sakkuth was another name for Moloch.

"Luck Theology" In The Promised Land Of Canaan

Did you bring to Me sacrifices and cereal offerings during those forty years in the wilderness, O house of Israel?

[No] but [instead of bringing Me the appointed sacrifices] you carried about the tent of your king Sakkuth and Kaiwan [names for the gods of the planet Saturn], your images of your star-god which you made for yourselves [and you will do so again].

Amos 5:25-26 *(The Amplified Bible)*

The prophet Amos delivered God's message to the ten northern tribes of Israel: "You have not worshipped Me, but have lifted up the tabernacle of Moloch, your star-king." Moloch was intimately connected with Taurus, the solar bull, and the planet Saturn.

The connection between the sun and Saturn probably arose from both being taken as symbols of Time. The return of the sun to the beginning of the zodiac marked the completion of the year. Saturn, the slowest moving of all the heavenly bodies, accomplished its revolution through the signs of the zodiac in about 30 years, a complete generation of men. Saturn therefore was in a peculiar sense the symbol of Time, and because of Time, of Destiny. [6]

Moloch became the Israelite's adopted god of **destiny**. It was to him they offered their sacrifices and made their request. They called on him for his protection. They believed this god of **fate** or **destiny** controlled major events surrounding their lives. They named him the determiner or the predestinator of their future.

⌘⌘⌘⌘

The ten northern tribes of Israel continued to practice Assyrian idolatry, prolifically. By the sixth century B.C., they had turned full force to popular Babylonian-Assyrian gods like Meni, another god of **destiny**, and Baal-Gad, a god of **fortune**, with which we are already familiar. A clear reference to this practice is pointed out by the following:

> But you who forsake the Lord, who forget *and*
> ignore My holy Mount [Zion], who prepare a
> table for Gad [the Babylonian god of fortune]
> and who furnish mixed drinks for Meni [the
> god of destiny].
>
> Isaiah 65:11 [*Amplified Bible*]

This record shows us how the ten northern tribes of Israel were not worshipping God in the "appointed place" of Jerusalem. They had abandoned the True God and were worshipping Babylonian –Assyrian **luck** gods instead. The Israelites no longer looked to God for prosperity and peace and purpose, rather they looked to Baal-Gad, the lord of good **fortune**. Baal-Gad worship was well established throughout the Near East in Isaiah's day. Even before Joshua's day, there was a well-known sight of worship in the land of Canaan, Cf., Joshua 11:17 and 12:7.

One practice in the worship of Baal-Gad was to spread a feast before this idol at the commencement of the new year in an effort to secure a blessing of prosperity. That is exactly the practice Isaiah describes. Israel was seeking a blessing of good **fortune** for the year from the hands of what we would call "good **luck** gods." The bogus concepts we are studying were fully embraced by the Israelites. They not only knew the meaning of **destiny** and **fortune**, they bowed to the deities they believed were controlling these categories.

Most of the pagan gods the Israelites worshipped were associated with stars, planets, and other heavenly bodies.

> Arabian tradition styled the planet Jupiter the greater fortune, and Venus the lesser fortune. Jewish tradition identified Gad with the planet Jupiter, and it has been conjectured that Meni is to be identified with the planet Venus. [7]

Yet another possibility is that Baal-Gad and Meni were associated with the Hyades and the Pleiades, the two beautiful star clusters located in Taurus, the Bull. [8]

The descriptive summary of 2 Kings 17, reveals the ruinous results of Israel's idolatrous **luck** god worship. The northern tribes of Israel fervently lusted after the popular deities associated with heavenly bodies. They worshipped the "host of heaven." They operated divination and enchantments to determine their **lot**. They deserted Jehovah God's blessings and protection; thereby they sold themselves into Assyrian captivity.

65

> And they left all the commandments of the
> Lord their God, and made them molten
> images, even two calves, and made a grove, and
> worshipped all the host of heaven, and served
> Baal.
>
> And they caused their sons and their daughters
> to pass through the fire [of Moloch], and used
> divination [**lot** casting] and enchantments, and
> sold themselves to do evil in the sight of the
> Lord, to provoke Him to anger.
>
> Therefore the Lord was very angry with Israel,
> and removed them out of His sight: there was
> none left but the tribe of Judah only.
>
> 2 Kings 17:16-18

Eventually, the southern tribe of Judah fell prey to the same enticing "luck theology" the ten northern tribes had earlier embraced. The last record we are going to review in this chapter is a reference to the Judean practice of star worship from the book of Jeremiah. The occurrence of this account is shortly after the destruction of Jerusalem by the Babylonian king, Nebuchadnezzar. The account reveals the perverted practice of attributing "good **fortune**" to still another star-god.

> But we will certainly do whatsoever thing goeth
> forth out of our own mouth, to burn incense
> unto the queen of heaven, and to pour out
> drink offerings unto her, as we have done, we,
> and our fathers, our kings, and our princes, in

the cities of Judah, and in the streets of Jerusalem: for *then* had we plenty of victuals [food], and were well, and saw no evil.

Jeremiah 44:17

The reference here is specifically to a group of Judean women who had escaped to Egypt from Babylonian destruction, and who were continuing to worship the "queen of heaven." The reference concerning the "queen of heaven" may refer to the Babylonian god Ishtar, a goddess of fertility, also identified with the planet Venus. [9]

These misguided Judean women were ascribing their plenty and well-being to this false goddess of **fortune**. They had forsaken Jehovah, God, their real protection and supply. They had sown the winds of idolatry and they were about to reap the whirlwind of disaster and emptiness (see Jeremiah 44:22 and 23).

By the fifth century B.C., the Israelites had lost their "wrestling match" with Assyrian "luck theology." They caved in to its absurd mentality and prostrated themselves before gods of **destiny** and **fortune**. They sided with the ambiguous logic of **luck**. The tremendous blessing and protection afforded them by Jehovah God they ascribed to Baal-Gad, Meni, Moloch, and Ishtar. What was the result of their wayward behavior? Their acceptance and practice of Assyrian "luck theology" led directly to their being carried to Assyria as captive slaves.

During the time frame we have considered, "luck theology" mushroomed. Men and women acknowledged and accepted bogus pagan beliefs. "Luck theologies" were thoroughly integrated into Eastern thinking and believing. All five of the companion terms that are used today in defining the modern idea of **luck** are traceable to early Eastern idolatrous belief.

We are cautioned in God's Word not to be so naïve and gullible when we are confronted with lying theologies.

> That we *henceforth* be no more children, tossed
> to and fro, and carried about with every wind
> of doctrine, by the sleight of men, *and* cunning
> craftiness whereby they lie in wait to deceive;
> Ephesians 4:14

The need is that we wake-up and stay alert to the serious ramifications of "luck theologies." Deceptive doctrines about **luck** are commonly embraced by our popular culture, but are we beginning to see how closely these ambiguous concepts are linked to pagan idolatry? These crafty, fictitious, lying concepts need to be avoided. We need to develop a more wholesome vocabulary.

> But speaking the truth in love, may grow up
> into him in all things, which is the head, *even*
> Christ:
> Ephesians 4:15

We must literally "hold on to our love of Truth." God's Word is Truth, and as we hold on to the Truth of God's Word by loving it and living it, we can grow up into Christ in all things.

The imperative need is that we set the Word of God above

every doctrine of man. We make God's Word the standard by which every precept must be judged. When we do so, we will not be "tossed to and fro and carried about by every wind of doctrine." We can refuse to be carried about by popular concepts like **luck** and **chance**, and all the other bogus terms we are studying! We need to operate spiritual discernment and see these lying concepts for what they are. They are actually distortions of truth conveyed by false theologies and myths. They are lies propounded by men of corrupt minds. We will see later that they are also devilish doctrines designed to undermine God's Word and His people.

Thus far, we have traced the commencement of "luck theology" to Nimrod and his descendants, the Babylonians. We have seen a little about how distorted pagan theologies developed, spread, and thrived throughout the Near East. We saw how Israel turned to worship Assyrian star-gods. They believed these gods were going to dole out their **fortune** and **fate**. They believed star-gods were controlling and determining their **lot** in life. Israel's idolatrous practice of worshipping gods of **destiny** and **fortune,** however, led to the destruction of their homeland, and ultimately to Assyrian and Babylonian captivity.

Time-wise now, we are going to move up to the third century B.C. We will see what the Greeks and Romans did with the concept of **luck.** We are going to see the names of some new false gods. However, we will learn these gods are not new, but are only old gods dressed up with new names. We will see how "luck theology" concepts move into their idolatrous cultures with little change. We will see how the Greek and Roman worlds embrace "luck theology," hook, line, and sinker. Just watch how they accept Eastern theologies and then advance them by their own inept brands of paganism.

No Such Thing As Luck

[1] Bulliger, E.W., *The Companion Bible*, Zondervan Bible Publishers, Grand Rapids, MI, 1974, Appendix 188, p. 208

[2] *The Encyclopedia Americana, Vol. 15*, Americana Corp., NY, 1963, p.411

[3] Waterson, Barbara, *The Gods of Ancient Egypt*, Facts on File Pub., NY, 1948, p. 124

[4] Bulliger, E.W., *The Witness of the Stars*, Kregel Pub., Grand Rapids, MI, 1967, p. 120

[5] *The International Standard Bible Encyclopedia, Vol. I*, Wm. B.Eerdmans Pub., Grand Rapids, MI, 1960, p. 298

[6] Ibid.

[7] *The International Standard Bible Encyclopedia, Vol. II*, Wm. B.Eerdmans Pub., Grand Rapids, MI, 1960, p. 1152

[8] Ibid., *Vol. I.*, p. 299

[9] *The Amplified Bible*, Zondervan Corp., USA, Ebt Frances Siewert, 1987, p. 1082 (footnote b)

CHAPTER FOUR

"Luck Theology"
in Greece and Rome

There is no need to spend a great deal of time working through the sordid, religious history of the ancient Greeks and Romans. We will only need to consider a limited number of their gods and goddesses to establish their attitude toward "luck theology."

> For the Jews require a sign, and the Greeks seek after wisdom:
>
> But we preach Christ crucified, unto the Jews a stumblingblock, and unto the Greeks foolishness;
> 1 Corinthians 1:22-23

With all of their "seeking after wisdom" the great Greek Empire showed very little of it by their worshipping gods of fate and goddesses of fortune. The weak moral structure of both the Greek and Roman Empires was the direct result of their worshipping idolatrous gods of every description. The vast array of their gods and goddesses formed a family of false deities. These gods, they believed, governed almost every aspect of life.

Over 2000 years have passed since these Empires flourished, but we still have their super, human-like idols and gods constantly thrown before our faces, as if they are worthy of valid consideration. When is it ever edifying to sort through the foolish theological beliefs of these lauded civilizations? A strange mixture of mythology and pagan idolatry captivated the mind-set of both these peoples. In order to understand their brands of idolatrous theology, it is helpful to know a little about their mythology.

Ancient authors of Greek, Roman, and Near-Eastern mythology were big contributors to the concepts of fate, fortune, and other "chance theologies." These authors assimilated pagan, idolatrous beliefs into their mythical narratives. They fostered and propagated idolatrous logic and helped it to live among their civilizations.

> Mythology comprises the description of the gods, their names, functions, and relationships, and the various stories, commonly called myths, told about gods and heroes.... The greatest role both in invention and transformation was played by the poets. [1]

Ancient poets and orators successfully produced what became a vast, sordid mythology. Their narratives helped to define the nature and characteristics of idolatrous gods. They laid the foundation upon which both Greek and Roman idolatry continued to prosper.

⌘⌘⌘⌘

Please be careful to observe that myths were only the surmising of people who were called poets, orators, and sometimes philosophers. Mythological authors were only people; with people imaginations, people conceptions, people aspirations, people beliefs, people delusions and people fears. Greek and Roman myths have no more credibility than the people who authored them.

So, how much reverence and credibility should we give to Greek and Roman myths? Still today, our school children are taught that myths are central to human experience. They are taught that myths explain how things came to be. Take a look at this quote from a current sixth grade *Elements of Literature* textbook.

> Myths may also explain such big questions as why we suffer, why seasons change, why a religious ritual is practiced, or what happens after death. These are serious matters, so it is wise to treat all myths with respect. [2]

Why would a board of education and a school administration allow this "stuff" in a sixth grade classroom? What we need to do for both our children and adults, is to

75

encourage them to treat myths for what they truly are. They are graphic distortions of reality, generally authored by God-rejecters, whose views of the important elements of life are actually perversions of Truth. Myths are generally bizarre tales that have no factual basis. Most of them openly pervert Truth and champion error and idolatrous falsehoods. (Later we will look, in greater detail, at other aspects of mythological influence.)

⌘⌘⌘⌘

The next thing we are going to consider is how the "homegrown" idolatry of the Greek World, mixed with that of the Near East World we studied in Chapters Two and Three. Greek conquest of the Near East led to the influence of Eastern thought. It is not that the Grecians needed Eastern influence to learn idolatry, for they knew that practice earlier. The point we need to consider here is that first the Greek, and later the Roman civilization, adopted and continued the Near East theology surrounding all five of the words we are studying. The following quote deals with the mixture of Greek and Eastern thought relative to the goddess Artemis.

> Later when Ephesus [a Near Eastern city] fell into the possession of the Greeks. Greek civilization partly supplanted the Asiatic, and in that city, the two civilizations were blended together. The Greek name of Artemis was given to the Asiatic goddess [Ishtar], and many of

the Greek colonists represented her on their coins as Greek. Her images and forms of worship remained more Asiatic than Greek." [3]

We know Artemis by her Roman name, Diana of the Ephesians. She is referred to by Demetrius, a silversmith, in the book of Acts. Speaking despairingly against the Apostle Paul's preaching of God's Word, Demetrius says:

> So that not only this our craft is in danger to be set at nought; but also that the temple of the great goddess Diana should be despised, and her magnificence should be destroyed, whom all Asia and the world worshippeth.
>
> Acts 19:27

All Asia had worshipped her for a span of at least a thousand years. By the time of the above reference, the first century A.D., all Asia was continuing to worship her. It is not difficult to trace Diana's origin, even though she was worshipped under different names in various parts of the Orient.

> "In Cappadocia she [Diana] was known as Ma; to the Syrians as Atargatis or Mylitta; among the Phoenicians as Astarte, a name which appears among the Assyrians as Ishtar: the modern name Esther is derived from it....The various goddesses of Syria and Asia Minor all owe their origin to the earlier Assyrian or Babylonian Ishtar." [4]

It is plain that both the Greeks and Romans assimilated many of the teachings and beliefs of the ancient Babylonian goddess, Ishtar. They practiced the same "luck theology" established earlier by the Babylonians. Although the Eastern theology remained the same, the Greeks called their goddess, Artemis. Eventually, in Roman times, her name was changed to Diana.

From the historical information we have of Diana, it is easy to see that she was associated with the "luck theology" we are studying. Two features about why she was worshipped are clear. One was fertility. She was worshipped as the universal mother of all creation. [5] A second feature of her worship involved the concept of **fate**. Women especially sought out this goddess as a protectress of their young. They believed she established and foretold the **fates** of their newborn children. [6]

⌘⌘⌘⌘

Diana was by no means the only ancient deity proclaimed to hold the power of **fate**. The Greek and Roman worlds were well supplied with gods and goddesses for any occasion. Today, practically everybody knows a little about the Greek god, Zeus. Among his supposed powers was the ability to control men and women. Humans could not resist him. Whatever Zeus determined about their lives came to pass. Humankind was bound by his will with no recourse. Zeus decided their **fate**. This was the mind-set of both the Greek and Roman worlds. Both of these famous civilizations bowed to this worthless, false god.

The Greek mythical "Moirai" may not be as well-known as Zeus. The Moirai were mythical sisters that were described as having the vast power to determine every human's **fate**. They are referred to often in Homer, Hesiod, and other mythical, literary works. [7] The teachings surrounding the Moirai sisters, or the "Fates", as they were called, will be discussed more fully in Chapter Five.

The concept of **chance** was established in the Greek goddess, "Tyche." The blessings of this goddess were thought to be whimsical and indefinite. She might bestow a benefit, but she could just as easily shed forth doom. The Greeks believed Tyche controlled both the aspects of **fortune** and **misfortune**.

> Tyche personified chance, good and bad, just or un-just, intervening in the fate of men or nations when she was able to change its course. [8]

The Greek word Tyche means **fortunate** or **chance**. The Romans adopted some of the concepts built around the Greek "Tyche," but they named their goddess, Fortuna. Our modern word "**fortune**" is derived from the concepts surrounding this Roman goddess.

> The goddess of blind Luck and Chance, she [Fortuna] offers mortals, according to her whims, wealth or poverty, power or subservience. Presiding over all of life's events, she holds all power over men. Holding a horn of plenty and a rudder: because she guides the affairs of the world. [9]

Fortuna is often pictured standing on a sphere or a wheel. So now we know where the "wheel of **fortune**" originated. (The popular game show, "Wheel of Fortune", has aired on television since 1979.)

No Such Thing As Luck

Hecate was still another Greek goddess thought to be a bestower of **fortune**. According to the *Concise Dictionary of Classical Mythology*:

> She extended her goodwill towards all mortals: she could grant material prosperity, eloquence in political assemblies, and victory in battle and sporting events. She had the power to give fishermen big hauls of fish, and she made cattle grow fat or lean at will. [10]

The Greeks believed that she presided over several categories of life including magic and spells.

The last "good **luck**" god we are going to deal with in this chapter is the Greek god, Hermes. The Romans changed his name to Mercury. They also changed the name of Zeus to Jupiter. Both gods, Jupiter and Mercury, are named in the following record.

> And there sat a certain man at Lystria, impotent in his feet, being a cripple from his mother's womb, who never had walked:
>
> The same heard Paul speak; who steadfastly beholding him, and perceiving that he had faith to be healed,
>
> Said with a loud voice, "Stand upright on thy feet." And he leaped and walked.
>
> And when the people saw what Paul had done, they lifted up their voices, saying in the speech of Lycaonia, The gods are come down to us in the likeness of men.

"Luck Theology" In Greece And Rome

And they called Barnabas, Jupiter; and Paul, Mercurius [Mercury], because he was the chief speaker.

Acts 14:8-12

Upon the occasion of the Apostle Paul healing this lame man in Lystra of Asia Minor, tremendous excitement erupted. The Lycaonian citizens of Lystra mistakenly ascribed this great miracle of healing to their gods, Jupiter and Mercury. They had witnessed the total restoration of a man lame from his birth. These Lycaonians immediately thought their gods had taken human form in the likeness of Paul and his fellow helper Barnabas.

> The Lycaonians were no doubt familiar with the legend [myth] of Jupiter and Mercury's visit in disguise to the aged couple, Philemon and Baucis, the scene of which was laid in the neighboring province of Phrygia. [11]

Ovid mythology portrays how the aged couple, Philemon and Baucis, were generously bestowed with favors as a result of having extended hospitality to these two gods which had taken human form and descended to Earth. These Lycaonian citizens believed this Ovid legend was happening again. The whole town was caught up in excitement and wonder. The citizens of this region, along with most of the Roman Empire, believed Jupiter and Mercury to be the rewarders and bestowers of good **fortune**. These Lycaonians thought they were witnessing a first-hand demonstration of it right before their very eyes. They believed Jupiter and Mercury had brought good **fortune** to this impotent man by healing him.

No Such Thing As Luck

The priests of these "good **luck**" gods were so convinced about this man's having been healed by Jupiter and Mercury, that they brought forth oxen and garlands to the gates of the city to offer sacrifices to Paul and Barnabas.

> *Which* when the apostles, Barnabas and Paul, heard *of*, they rent their clothes, and ran in among the people, crying out,
>
> And saying, "Sirs, why do ye these things? We also are men of like passions with you, and preach unto you that ye should turn from these vanities unto the living God, Which made heaven, and earth, and the sea, and all things that are therein:"
>
> Acts 14:14-15

Paul and Barnabas could barely restrain these people from their offering of sacrifices. Paul began to urge the Lycaonians to stop this vanity. He encouraged them to turn away from their vain worship of Jupiter and Mercury. He pointed them to the LIVING God. They were encouraged to turn their confidence to the True God of heaven and earth. It was by God's power the lame man was healed. The Apostle Paul did persuade a few of these men and women to turn from their idolatry. However, some of these hard-hearted Lycaonians later turned against Paul and stoned him. (Perhaps it was by the same gate where they had earlier tried to offer sacrifices to him.)

"Luck Theology" In Greece And Rome

⌘⌘⌘⌘

Before ending this chapter, we are going to look at another record from the book of Acts. This record allows us to grasp, in vivid detail, the Greek and Roman world's gullible attitude toward idolatry; idolatry which successfully kept "luck theology" alive and growing. It may be a little hard for us to comprehend how extensively idolatrous practices flourished in Athens and the entire Greco-Roman world. (A good comparison might be the extensive number of denominational church buildings found in most any American city today.) There were no holds barred, and generally no religious boundaries in this ancient city. Most of the people in first century Athens were devoted to strange, human-like gods. They were somewhat like those described in 2 Timothy 3:7, "Ever learning, and never able to come to the knowledge of the truth."

In first century Athens, amidst all the vast and conflicting theology and philosophy which ruled that city, a man of God stood up and proclaimed the accuracy of God's Word. When the Apostle Paul entered into the city of Athens this is what ensued:

> Now while Paul waited for them [his fellow-helpers] at Athens, his spirit was stirred in him, when he saw the city wholly given to idolatry.
>
> Therefore disputed he in the synagogue with the Jews, and with the devout persons, and in the market daily with them that met with him.

83

Then certain philosophers of the Epicureans,
and of the Stoicks encountered him. And some
said, "What will this babbler say?" other some,
"He seemeth to be a setter forth of strange
gods:" because he preached unto them
Jesus, and the resurrection.

And they took him, and brought him unto
Areopagus [Mars Hill], saying, "May we know
what this new doctrine, whereof thou speakest,
is?

For thou bringest certain strange things to our
ears: we would know therefore what these
things mean."

(For all the Athenians and strangers which were
there spent their time in nothing else, but either
to tell, or to hear some new thing.)

                              Acts 17:16-21

These Athenians were ever learning something new. That
was the way they spent much of their time. However, the
philosophies of the Epicureans and Stoics were not new.
Extensive philosophical teachings about life had been
floating around Athens for hundreds of years. Plato and
earlier Greek philosophers had heaped and spouted their
thinking upon the Greek people for generations. The
development of philosophical systems by numerous schools
of Greek thought appears to be a type of rebellion against
religion. These schools of thought were attempting to present
a new and different alternative to idolatrous religions. Their
philosophical methods for reaching conclusions rested upon
the human intellect. In effect, they were saying, "No need

for the gods; we have the capacity to figure out life on our own." By Paul's day, this glorying in human reasoning stood on an equal footing with idolatrous theologies. It is no surprise that Athenian philosophers wanted to hear Paul's reasoning. They were interested in his reasoning, but the vast numbers of them were not interested in his God. As a matter of fact, most all of them rejected God.

Exalted human reasoning continues to reject God and His Wonderful Word.

> For after that in the wisdom of God the world
> by wisdom knew not God, it pleased God by
> the foolishness of preaching to save them that
> believe.
>
> 1 Corinthians 1:21

Human reasoning makes room for bogus philosophies and theologies. Human reasoning makes room for the concept of **luck** and "luck theology." Human reasoning accepts fatalistic doctrines. The natural mind of man is a superstitious mind; and, the natural mind of man is enmity against the things of God!

Paul's preaching of God's Word brought truth to the hearing of these "home-spun" Athenian philosophers.

> Then Paul stood in the midst of Mars' hill, and
> said, "Ye men of Athens, I perceive that in all
> things ye are too superstitious [religious].
>
> For as I passed by, and beheld your devotions,
> I found an altar with this inscription, TO THE
> UNKNOWN GOD. Whom therefore ye
> ignorantly worship, Him declare I unto you.

No Such Thing As Luck

God that made the world and all things therein, seeing that He is Lord of heaven and earth, dwelleth not in temples made with hands;

Neither is worshipped with men's hands, as though He needed any thing, seeing He giveth to all life, and breath, and all things;

And hath made of one blood all nations of men for to dwell on all the face of the earth, and hath determined the times before appointed, and the bounds of their habitation;

That they should seek the Lord, if haply they might feel after Him, and find Him, though He be not far from every one of us:

For in Him we live, and move, and have our being; as certain also of your own poets have said, 'For we are also His offspring.'

Forasmuch then as we are the offspring of God, we ought not to think that the Godhead is like unto gold, or silver, or stone, graven by art and man's device.

And the times of this ignorance God winked at; but now commandeth all men every where to repent:

Because He hath appointed a day, in the which He will judge the world in righteousness by *that* man whom He hath ordained; *whereof* He hath given assurance unto all *men,* in that He hath raised him from the dead."

And when they heard of the resurrection of the dead, some mocked: and others said, "We will hear thee again of this *matter.*"

Acts 17:22-32

Paul fearlessly stood up before these critical Athenians that day with the power of God fully evident in his life. He proclaimed the power of the Gospel to those "puffed-up" Athenians: power that could bring deliverance for their lives and set them free. He confronted their idolatry. He taught them about the True God, the maker of life and breath, and all things. The True God did not need their temples, their shrines, and the work of their hands.

It was time for these men of Athens to turn from their pagan worship, to worship the God and Father of our Lord, Jesus Christ. God had raised His Son Jesus Christ from the dead, and this resurrection brought eternal life to any man who would believe. On the basis of Jesus Christ's standard of righteousness the future judgment of the world would come to pass. However, the vast number of these high-sounding philosophers and public officials rejected God's Word; some mocked and others of them delayed. There were only a few Athenians who believed Paul's preaching of the Gospel that day. Although few believed Paul's preaching in Athens, a great number of the Greek people did eventually turn from pagan idolatries. A testimony of praise about the Thessalonian Christian Church from that region is as follows:

No Such Thing As Luck

> How ye turned to God from idols to serve the
> living and true God;
>
> 1 Thessalonians 1:9b

These Thessalonians, and many others among the Greeks,
turned away from false, lifeless idols to serve a true and living
God.

⌘⌘⌘⌘

It is almost unbelievable that something so outrageous
as the bogus concepts of **fate, destiny, lot, fortune,** and
chance could spread and thrive the way they did. From their
Babylonian beginnings, all of these fatalistic doctrines
traveled by way of idolatry into the Greek and Roman worlds.
"Chance Theologies" were broadly accepted and assimilated
into their cultures. The idolatrous practices of these two
nations abounded throughout their long histories. Their
poets and orators enlarged doctrines related to **fate** and
fortune. Philosophers, with their worldly wisdom, often
perpetuated the identical reasoning. Perhaps these ancient
civilizations are remembered most for their outlandish
religious logic. But, doesn't much of their idolatrous logic
remain current? Actually, it does!

We have surveyed only a few of the idols of the ancient
Greek and Roman worlds. The *New Larousse Encyclopedia of
Mythology* lists several hundreds of their gods and goddesses.[12]
The most noteworthy characteristic, common to them all,
centers upon their presumed ability to influence and control
human life. Looking from a broader perspective, all of their

gods and goddesses functioned upon the basis of deterministic theologies of one sort or another. The pivotal point of both Greek and Roman religious devotions centered on beliefs involving **fate**'s doom and **fortune**'s blessings. They fully established these idolatrous ideas.

The Greek and Roman Empires passed away long ago, but the "luck theologies" they practiced and enlarged have not passed away. These very concepts live among us today! Since the fall of Rome, poets, orators, and philosophers have continued to declare the same bogus notions. What they have written in the last 1600 years continues to nurture the uncanny belief systems of ancient "luck theologies". They have declared a great deal about these concepts, but they have added little that is new. Therefore, there is no profit in surveying what they have written. For our purposes, it would be a waste of effort and space.

From time to time, throughout the centuries, a few individuals have confronted and withstood the deep-rooted doctrines of "luck theologies." Their influence, however, has failed to register with the masses. The concepts of **fate, destiny, lot, fortune,** and **chance** continue to be relentlessly proclaimed before us. These worthless belief systems enjoy a worldwide influence, but that influence needs to be aggressively confronted. Because this is true, we need to accurately define each of these concepts individually. A fuller definition of these words not only needs to be studied but understood with some depth. Chapter Five will begin to deal with a complete and fuller definition for the concept of **fate**.

No Such Thing As Luck

[1] *The Encyclopedia Americana*, Vol. 13, Americana Corp., NY., 1963, p.419b

[2] *6 Elements of Literature (Introductory Course)*, Holt, Rinehart and Winston, NY, 1997, special contribution by Joseph Brachac, p.198

[3] Orr, James, *The International Standard Bible Encyclopedia*, Wm. B. Eerdmans Publishing Co., Grand Rapids MI, 1974, p. 1631

[4] Ibid.

[5] Bulliger, E.W., *The Companion Bible*, Zondervan Bible Pub., Grand Rapids, MI., 1974, p. 1631

[6] *Larousse Encyclopedia of Mythology*, Ed. Robert Graves, Prometheus Press, NY, 1959, p. 223

[7] *The Encyclopedia Americana*, Vol.19, Americana Corp., NY, 1963, p.310

[8] Schmidt, Joel, *Larousse Greek and Roman Mythology*, McGraw Hill Book Co., NY, 1959, p. 223

[9] Ibid., p. 107

[10] Grimal, Pierre, *Concise Dictionary of Classical Mythology*, Basil Blackwell Publishing, Cambridge, Mass., 1986, p. 171

[11] Bulliger, p. 1614

[12] *New Larousse Encyclopedia of Mythology*, Introduction by Robert Graves, Hamlyn Publishing Co., NY, 1977

Fate is nothing more than the groundless reasoning of men who falsely claim that a certain force, the force of a god, has the ability to control human life.

CHAPTER FIVE

"Fickled" Fate

Mythical references to the supposed powers of pagan gods and goddesses form the foundation upon which the idea of **fate** has rested through the centuries of history. **Fate** is the first of the five "luck theology" concepts we are going to examine closely. **Destiny, lot, fortune,** and **chance** will follow in succeeding chapters. Along the way, through these chapters, we will take the time to look at other words that are related to this study. You may need a clothespin for your nose and hip boots for your feet and legs as we wade into the slimy thinking that has produced the concept of **fate** and the other terms we are going to study. Bring both of them along just in case.

Few people challenge the meaning of **fate.** Common acceptance of the idea has legitimized the word. It is long overdue that we take a serious look at the ramifications of what **fate** is all about. What do you personally understand about **fate,** and how does this concept fit into your life? Do you believe your life has been influenced in some way by a force of **fate**? Maybe you have been conditioned to think **fate** is a perfectly normal word to use, but it is not. It is interesting to note, according to *Webster's Dictionary*, the Old English synonym for **fate** is "weird," and this is exactly where the concept of **fate** belongs. It absolutely belongs in the category of the weird. It is suggestive of something mysterious, eerie, and odd. The fundamental idea of **fate** is that of a mysterious, supernatural power acting upon our lives.

Fate is often referred to as a "power of determination." This supposed power of **fate** exists somewhere in the heavens, but hovers beyond our sight. It is said to possess the uncanny ability to act upon us by overstepping our ability to determine our personal future. This (supposedly) "great power of determination" cancels out our individual freedom of will, and we have no choice. We must submit to it. According to its popular concept, **fate's** power literally takes away our freedom to act. **Fate** stands in opposition to freedom. All of these weird ideas are precepts associated with **fate.**

Sadly, far too many have bought into the phony, groundless logic of **fate**. You and I constantly hear misguided references to what has been caused by this counterfeit power. Phrases like, "as **fate** would have it," or "a twist of **fate**," are commonplace. Often people are driven by the belief that **fate** has called them to success and even greatness. Others consider themselves to be paralyzed by what **fate** has adversely decreed. The doctrine of fatalism is predicated upon the premise that individual freedom must give way to a fixed and inevitable **destiny**. We constantly hear the fatalistic excuses of individuals that embrace such logic. They are too quick to abandon their personal responsibilities, and lay the blame for failure at **fate's** door.

⌘⌘⌘⌘

We are going to look at three separate dictionary definitions for **fate**. By taking the time to wade through all three of these definitions, we can grasp the fuller meaning behind **fate's** concept.

Webster's New World Dictionary:
Fate
(1)   The power supposed to determine the outcome of events before they occur;
(2)   Something inevitable supposedly determined by this power; hence
(3)   What happens or has happened to a person; lot; fortune: as, it was his *fate* to be a bachelor.
SYN.- fate refers to the inevitability of a course of events as supposedly predetermined by a god or other agency beyond human control. [1]

The Barnhart Dictionary of Etymology:
Fate
From L. fãtum, things spoken (by the gods) one's destiny, from neuter past partec: plu. of fãri speak; the source of power supposed to control what happens. [2]

No Such Thing As Luck

The Oxford English Dictionary:
Fate
The primary sense of the Latin word is a sentence or doom of the gods; but it was subsequently used as the equivalent of the Gr. *Moira*, which, originally meaning only a person's 'lot' or 'portion', had come to express the more abstract conception explained below:
(1)   The principle, power, or agency by which, according to certain philosophical and popular systems of belief, all events, or some events in particular, are unalterably predetermined from eternity.
(2)   Mythol.   a. The goddess of fate or destiny; in Homer *Moira*. b. *pl.* In later Greek and Roman mythology, the three goddesses supposed to determine the course of human life (Gr. *Moirai* L. *Parcae, Fata*). [3]

The key elements in the idea of **fate** are easy to summarize: that which is predetermined, declared and actuated by a god or gods upon life. A god, who is always the central acting force, is believed by some to have the power to predetermine a future outcome. Next, that god speaks forth or declares his will. Lastly, people and events are locked-in and controlled by the god's power and what has been proclaimed will thusly come to pass. There is nothing more to it; that's all there is!

The key elements listed by our dictionaries only reflect what mythology first described about **fate** long ago. Nothing essential to **fate's** original inception is missing. The concept has successfully traveled through centuries of time to our day unscathed, untarnished and unchanged. The meaning of **fate**, however, will not escape the confines of this chapter unchallenged!

⌘⌘⌘⌘

The *Oxford English Dictionary's* reference to the goddess of **fate** and **destiny** needs a fuller discussion. The original, pinpoint commencement of fatalistic belief was conceived by the corrupted minds of men who rejected God and His Word. Some of these God-rejecting men claimed their idolatrous gods, had the power to control the universe and also their lives individually.

Authors of mythology have written prolifically about the imagined powers of the same false gods. They successfully incorporated the stupidity of pagan theological beliefs into their mythical narratives. In effect, they have relayed to us the absurd, pagan logic and belief, which personally influenced their thinking. We have limited documentation to clarify the actual ritual and practices involved in the worship of ancient gods. Today however, much of what is believed about ancient gods comes directly from mythological authorship. This is essentially true of **fate**.

Among the assumed powers of mythological gods and goddesses, the power of **fate** ruled supreme. Practically all pagan gods are described as having this paralyzing power to control humans, but usually in varying degrees. The god, Zeus, is said to have had the greatest power. He could decree the **fate** of both men and even lesser gods. However, according to mythical reasoning, above all the gods, and even Zeus, stood **"The Fates."**

No Such Thing As Luck

It is by the collective literatures of Hosiad, Homer, and other ancient authors, that **fate's** meaning has been established. Mythology's authorship actually believed in **fate's** reality, and they defined its function. Their penmanship defined how **fate** worked and what it did. Their mythological writings described what they believed concerning their huge family of gods and goddesses. They described how these deities possessed **fate's** power and how they used it. Whether from **"The Fates"** or by the decree of a god, **fate** is described as being cast upon men and women to control and limit their lives.

The *Larousse Encyclopedia of Mythology* describes **The Fates** as follows:

> They were three in number, daughters of Night, and they were called: Clotho, Lachesis and Atropos. Clotho, the spinner, personified the thread of life. Only in Hesiod's *Theogony* are they treated as goddesses. Lachesis was chance, the element of luck that a man had the right to expect. Atropos was inescapable fate, against which there was no appeal. The whole of man's life was shadowed by the Fates. They arrived at his birth with Ilithyia. When he was married the three Fates had to be invoked so that the union should be happy. And when the end approached the Fates hastened to cut the thread of his life. [4]

Hesiod's *Theogony* calls these sisters goddesses. To Homer they are portrayed as bestowing a gripping **destiny**.

These poorly defined, mystical sisters are described as having the power to control the **fate** of every earthly and heavenly creature, and their power was assumed to be absolute. Mythical references to **The Fates** describe how they possessed great omniscience. Their all-knowing eyes could scan the future of mortals. Whatever they proclaimed about the future was going to come to pass. That is how they were perceived.

⌘⌘⌘⌘

Through the ages, many have presumed the existence of **fate**. What mythology established about the idea of **fate**, early philosophers tried to clarify and enlarge.

> Plato gathered myths and beliefs concerning Fate, and reshaped them in a certain order which was to be adhered to closely by subsequent thinkers. In his works, therefore, we can establish the stage and the implications which had been reached concerning Fate and its relation to Fortune. [5]

> Aristotle analyzes the realm of Fortune in terms often repeated in the Middle Ages, and which explains the many later usages of Fortune, Fate, and Chance. [6]

No Such Thing As Luck

Early philosophers bolstered the credibility of **fate** and **fortune's** meaning. Many early thinkers verified mythological concepts by attempting to personally define them. In their vain attempts to define something they believed to exist, (but which in reality does not exist), they helped "luck theology" survive. They also helped to substantiate and certify the vocabulary by which "luck theology" continues to thrive and to live in the minds of men today.

Philosophers and theologians continued, all along in history, to redefine **fate's** meaning. They called it by several new names, including some of the following. **Fate** has been called: indeterminism and the law of nature – natural necessity – causal necessity – providence and – the order and connection of all causes inherent in the universe. They have said **fate** operates independent of reason and nature. They have said it operates through personal instinct. They have claimed **fate** is a cause unknown to human understanding. Others have said **fate** equals the sum total of principle causes. [7]

Through the ages, men such as Democritus, Aristotle, Apuleius, Chalcidius, Augustine, Saint Thomas of Aquinas, Boethius, Machiavelli, and a host of others, have tried to explain **fate's** true meaning. They have hammered and tried to reshape it. They have symbolized and personified it. They have taught of its morality and its lack thereof. They have taught how to escape it and also how providential care includes it. But none of these men established and confirmed **fate's** reality; they only talked about it! Augustine entered this senseless discussion of **fate** by trying to explain why terms like **fate, fortune** and **chance** exist. His view that the order of the universe might well be called **Fate**, and thusly Providence, was a step in the wrong direction. But, he stood on sure ground when he stated that the word **fate** is misused and that, in fact, God is over all. [8]

⌘⌘⌘⌘

Early philosophers were not the only group to assume the existence of **fate**. Throughout history, God-rejecters have been quick to assume **fate**. They have subsequently, by leaving God out of their thoughts, maintained big vacuums in their understanding. They have wavered back and forth between the elusive doctrines and theories of men. They have clutched and grasped to the unsubstantiated and the erring, and have been enticed by the groundless reasoning of others. They have been among the superstitious, the prideful, and the foolish, and today they continue to confess the idolatrous logic of **fate**.

> The fool has said in his heart there is no God.
> Psalms 14:1a

Today, the "down-and-outers," who see themselves as being left behind, often blame **fate** for their condition. People who just do not understand why they have lost in life, why they do not share in the blessing and plenty of life, why they suffer, and why life has pushed them around, justify and explain their condition to be caused by **fate's** heavy-handed decree. Their confession and excuse is, "this supernatural power of determination is greater than my ability and capacity to do anything about it." They name themselves victims, and **fate** the aggressor. They claim innocence for themselves and quickly lay the blame for their dilemma upon **fate**. What a cop-out! What a transfer of responsibility! Their misguided conclusions are like that of a criminal who stands before the judge for his crime and explains his condition to be a work of **fate**. But in reality, the judge is going to hand down a sentence prescribed by law, no matter whom the man standing before him. The criminal may lay the blame for his condition upon **fate,** but the criminal's sentence is one of law, not of **fate**.

In this modern age, the assumed force of **fate** remains a weak, preposterous explanation for the causes behind our lives; "what has **fate** ever caused?" **Fate** is absolutely contrary to personal experience. We are not puppets on a string. Experience has taught us that personal responsibility determines the outcomes in our lives. For instance:

♦ slack efforts produce – poor results

♦ lazy slothful work habits – keep a man poor

♦ reckless, loose living produces — poverty and want

None of this has anything to do with the force of a god called **Fate**. Rather, the cause has to do with what an individual has chosen to do or not to do. If the individual chooses to remain idle and to live loosely, his condition is a direct reflection of his decisions. If this is an honest man, he knows in his heart-of-hearts, **fate** had nothing to do with his predicament. But, on the other hand, if this man seeks to shift the responsibility for his personal condition, he can blame the supposed force, called **fate**.

Personal experience countermands the idea of **fate**. There has never been a logical basis upon which the concept of **fate** can rest. We really know, if we are honest, exactly what we have chosen to do or not to do. And we also know that, in the end, we must live by our choices. By our own volition, we choose what to believe. We alone adapt and embrace the standards and precepts upon which our belief systems are founded. We can choose to adapt the truthful standard of God's Word, or we can choose a lesser standard. The sound standard for truth is the Living Word of God. The choosing of a lesser standard makes room for the idolatrous logic of **fate**.

⌘⌘⌘⌘

The ideology of **fate** has always been contrary to God's Word. The Bible does not contain a single reference to this word, nor does it substantiate the concept. However, even though the Bible does not refer to **fate** directly, biblical pertinence is essential to our understanding of how this idolatrous concept is detrimental. Over and over again, God's Word warns against the unfruitful practice of calling upon false gods.

In the Bible, false gods are described as having no wills, no power, and lacking the ability to do anything.

> Their idols *are* silver and gold, the work of men's hands.
>
> They have mouths, but they speak not: eyes have they, but they see not:

> They have ears, but they hear not: noses have they, but they smell not:
>
> They have hands, but they handle not: feet have they, but they walk not: neither speak they through their throat.
>
> They that make them are like unto them; *so is* every one that trusteth in them.
>
> Psalm 115:4-8

Biblical records plainly show how kingdoms and individuals were lifted up or cast down, based upon their allegiance to the True God or to false idolatrous gods. The Bible also describes the foundless devotion of godless men; men who groundlessly subjected themselves to idolatrous gods. It is the mythological descriptions of these false gods that has produced the "fickled" idea of **fate**. Again, **fate** is nothing more than the groundless reasoning of men who falsely claim that a certain force, the force of a god, has the ability to control human life.

⌘⌘⌘⌘

The general public carelessly claims **fate** to be the determining cause responsible for many of the abnormal events affecting their lives. An example that echoes the common belief and logic of our day can be found in the words of a New York fire fighter who escaped the disastrous collapse of the World Trade Center on 9-11-01. He is quoted to have given the following explanation for having escaped this disaster with his life.

> Sometimes when you see the building come
> down, it's like amazing I did not get killed— I
> didn't die, didn't get a scratch. It's just fate. [9]

Obviously, this brave man mistakenly credited to **fate** what
was in reality God's out-stretched hand of deliverance. Simply
pick up a newspaper and take a look! There you will read
how people frequently name **fate** to be the cause behind
numerous events.

News journalists frequently name **fate** to be the
determining cause behind the events they are reporting. For
example, look at the November 22, 2002 *Associated Press*
article reporting on the Fort Lauderdale, Florida jury trial of
a man charged with manslaughter. The headline caption
reads, "Jury deciding fate of ex-FBI agent in I-95 crash goes
home for night." The journalist who wrote this piece ascribed
the power of **fate** to the jury sitting on the case. What any
jury really decides, is guilt or innocence. Its decision has
nothing whatsoever to do with the power of **fate**.

Another article by the *Associated Press* (May 2, 2004
Floridan) displayed the following caption in bold half-inch
print:

Winn Dixie cutting back
fate of local store unknown

Actually, the article itself had nothing to do with an issue of **fate**. It dealt with the company's existing strategic plan to sell or close 150 of their grocery stores. The caption for this article, however, referred to the decision of whether to sell or close a local store as a determination of **fate**. The company executives of Winn-Dixie Stores Inc. would be quick to disavow the operation of **fate** in their decision. Obviously, profit or loss formed the framework of their decision.

⌘⌘⌘⌘

When it comes to determining reality beyond the five senses, worldly-minded people often turn to ridiculous, weird explanations, including the concept of **fate**. To understand dynamic causes that are beyond the capacity of our five senses requires spiritual perception and awareness. Men and women who are born of God's spirit have the ability to discern spiritual matters. They have body and soul, but they also have holy spirit life. Because they have spirit, they can discern spiritual matters. The worldly-minded or natural man of body and soul can not understand spiritual matters, essentially because they are foolishness to his thinking.

> But the natural man receiveth not the things
> of the Spirit of God: for they are foolishness
> unto him: neither can he know them, because
> they are spiritually discerned.
>
> 1 Corinthians 2:14

The natural-minded simply do not have the capacity to judge the spiritual aspects of life. It is this huge gap of spiritual understanding that has led to the unfounded logic and belief that surrounds **fate's** meaning.

The general public is not alone in its misguided conceptions of **fate**. Much of secular scholarship embraces a "luck theology" mentality that promotes the concept. The October 2002 *Reader's Digest* article, "Lucky You", by Marc Myers, attempts to describe the seven secrets of **lucky** people. The article includes the advice and instruction of five university professors of psychology and psychiatry, two professors of education, a sales executive and an author. (At this point you might want to question why professional men and women of learning and stature would choose to be associated with an article about the seven secrets of **lucky** people. At the very least, you might expect sound advice from people of such stature.) Take a good look at their quotes in "Lucky You." Look at their misguided logic and belief about **fate** and **luck** (it stands out like a sore thumb). They say:

> "Assume fate is on your side," "people who seem lucky are appealing because they are effective and happy," "I believe in fate, but I also believe you make your luck if you're open to new experiences," "sociability, energy and openness breed luck," "think lucky and you are more likely to be lucky," "you have to embrace random events that happen to you and see their potential for improving your luck." [10]

These conclusions fall well below the standard of sound judgment.

No Such Thing As Luck

Credentials of scholarship by the professionals who gave their advice in Marc Myers' article, stand without question. However, it is not scholarship that will determine the error of **fate**. The subject of **fate** needs to be examined from a spiritual perspective. Prideful, secular scholarship remains ignorant of spiritual matters. They egotistically claim the authority of their intelligence and education for soundness of judgment. Lacking the ability to discern spiritual matters and spiritual causes, they consistently reach faulty conclusions. They have done so with the pagan theological category; a category that definitely includes the ambiguous concept of **fate**. A confession of belief in **fate's** power remains a demonstration of misguided ignorance. Such a belief remains a failure to take into account the actual spiritual forces that do influence life.

⌘⌘⌘⌘

To comprehend the spiritual significance behind **fate's** development and why the concept remains active today, it is essential to understand that there are two spiritual powers alive and operating in the world. The Bible teaches there are two gods acting in the universe and influencing the world and everyone in it. Again, there are two and only two spiritual powers, and besides these, there are no others. It is true that there are lesser spirit beings, but they serve the purposes of either one or the other of these two gods.

The first ultimate spiritual power is the True God, our Heavenly Father. He is Spirit.

God is a Spirit: and they that worship Him
must worship *Him* in spirit and in truth.
John 4:24

He is the God and Father of our Lord, Jesus Christ, and He is
the beginning and the end. He is the creator of heaven and
earth. He is unlimited, and is exalted over all. He also loves
and cares for us individually.

The second spirit power is the devil, who is called Satan
and the Adversary. In the Bible, he is called the god of this
world.

But if our gospel be hid, it is hid to them that
are lost;

In whom the god of this world hath blinded
the minds of them which believe not, lest the
light of the glorious gospel of Christ, who is
the image of God, should shine unto them.
2 Corinthians 4: 3-4

The Devil is a spirit being but limited in scope and power.
He is the archenemy of the True God, and actively seeks to
replace Him. Jesus Christ described him as follows:

The thief [the Devil] cometh not, but for to
steal, and to kill, and to destroy:
John 10:10a

He is also rightfully called the Adversary and the Destroyer.

No Such Thing As Luck

This Adversary has, throughout human history, tried to destroy the sound doctrine of God's Word and to blind the minds of men to that Word. He stands in opposition to God and God's people. His purpose is to defeat God and the people of God. He can and does take control of human faculties by means of devil spirit possession.

⌘⌘⌘⌘

A devil spirit is able to gain control by alluring and persuading an individual to accept his presence, his nature, and his works. When an individual allows the cunning entrapments of a devil spirit to take root in his life, devil spirit possession can occur. The devil spirit possessed man has relinquished his ability to choose. When this happens, the possessing spirit exercises and manipulates the mental processes of the individual, thusly controlling and using him. Such a man is literally possessed; he is under the power and control of a devil spirit.

Maybe you have never associated devil spirit possession with the idea of **fate**; however, they are very much connected. When men abandoned the glory of the incorruptible God and sought to glorify the gods they themselves had made, the devil gained an opening through which he could work his purposes. The idolatrous gods of antiquity were completely without power. They were not capable of possessing or controlling anyone or anything. But, in contrast to man-made gods, devil spirits can and do possess human individuals who yield to their control.

The Devil seeks to conceal his nature and his works. His

mode of operation is secrecy. By means of implication, suggestion, and deception, he has successfully transferred his possessing characteristics to the so-called gods of **fate**. He has done so by subtly ascribing his works and his nature to them. He has purposefully cast his nature upon idolatrous gods and proclaimed that they have his "power to possess and control." His lying suggestion is: "the gods of this world can and do determine the outcomes in our lives." It is by this crafty disguise and lying deception, that the Adversary cloaks his works. He has people actually thinking and believing that it is the "power of **fate**" that does the possessing and the controlling. The devil has successfully deceived people into believing that human life can be controlled by supposed powers, which actually <u>do</u> <u>not</u> <u>exist</u>.

The two big essential claims in teachings about **fate** are that this power exists in reality, and it has the ability to control life. But **fate** has never existed. It has never had the power to control anything. It has never controlled a single human life. It is devil spirits, not **fate**, which can – and - do take control and possession of the yielding and unsuspecting human mind.

Proclamations about the "power of **fate**" draws and attracts men. They call for their attention and their interest. The concept itself has become a means of devilish allurement. It asks for a confession of belief. When men approach the idolatrous concept of **fate** and bow down to its proclaimed power, devil spirit possession is close at hand. You can count on it. Mental devotion to the idea of **fate**, and confession of belief in **fate's** power, are ways that provide an opening for the devil to "move in and set up housekeeping." That is what he can and will do to the unsuspecting human mind that is off-guard to his works. Such a confession is serious business. This is not a matter to be toyed with. The negative

111

confession that, "something up there can limit and control my life", is an open invitation for evil spirits to move into a human's mind.

> But those things which proceed out of the mouth come forth from the heart; and they defile the man.
>
> Matthew 15:18

> For by thy words thou shalt be justified, and by thy words thou shalt be condemned.
>
> Matthew 12:37

Idolatry has always provided a broad thoroughfare by which satanic influence has traveled directly into the human mind. A fruit of idolatry is devil spirit possession. The idolatrous mind is a fertile mind; a mind opened to devil spirit possession and control.

The devil happily promotes the concept of **fate**. He does his best to keep it lively and believable. Preposterous, lying doctrines about **fate** are designed to make the concept seem credible; but such doctrines foster copped –out excuses and crutches for men to lean upon. They promote the idea that a man's free will counts for little or nothing up against this (supposed) great power. The devil's false claim remains, "Some power, other than himself, does the possessing." What a joke!

⌘⌘⌘⌘

A related doctrine seeks to ascribe to God, Himself, the satanic nature that possesses and controls. This doctrine falsely teaches that God takes control of men and women and uses them for His purposes. Maybe you have heard people confess: "the spirit [God] moved me; or let the spirit [God] take control; or, God took away my desire to smoke." None of this is true. The True God never possesses men and women. He designed our freedom to choose. Why would He overstep it?

God has never violated anyone's freedom of will. He does not control us or force us; the opposite is true. Emphatically, in God's Word we are taught, over and over again, how God acts toward us. God's great love, mercy, and forgiveness woos us to submit to Him. His love and boundless grace wins our hearts. Force and control of human faculties is not from the True God; our Heavenly Father.

We freely give our love and loyalty to God because "He first loved us". We gladly do so! We rejoice in His love for us and in His goodness toward us. We praise Him and thank Him for the power He has given us, and for the peace of Christ which is shed upon our lives. What a God! What a Savior!

God desires our love and obedience, but He leaves our response to His love and grace up to us. It is for no other reason but our deliberate choice that we love God. We personally choose to love Him. That is the way God wants it to be. He is pleased when we respond to His love by loving

Him in return. This is the way God has arranged life at its best. It is called fellowship; God shares fully with us, and in response, we share fully with Him. This is the fullness of life and living, and there is no greater prize available here on earth.

⌘⌘⌘⌘

It is essential for us to understand that the Adversary does not have power over God's people unless they allow it. Additionally, the dark concept of **fate** must become dust under the Christian Believer's feet.

> Ye are of God, little children, and have overcome them: because greater is He [God] that is in you, than he [the devil and his devil spirits] that is in the world.
>
> 1 John 4:4

The Christian Believer should have no problem recognizing the doctrines that surround **fate** for what they are. We must not be taken in and deceived by false theologies. To do so will rob us of both our power and our peace. False theologies are always floating around, and they are designed to blind and deceive. The Christian Believer must absolutely remember that God's Wonderful Word is the perfect standard by which to judge truth and error, right and wrong, good and bad. The mature Believer, the understanding Believer, will not allow anything to come between himself and his wonderful God and Heavenly Father. For to walk in fellowship with God means great joy and peace and power.

The ideas of **fate**, and the doctrines that surround the concept, are simply not true. Anemic thought about **fate** is far removed from reality. God is real and to be praised! God is real and to be loved. His Word gives us clarity, enlightenment, and understanding. His Word makes no room for the concept of **fate** or any other fictitious power to rule over the hearts and lives of His people. By manifesting the power and love of God in our lives, we can walk victoriously over the "wiles of the Devil" and any lying doctrines which seek to verify the meaning of **fate**.

[1] *Webster's New World Dictionary*, World Pub., NY, 1968, s.v. "fate"

[2] *The Barnhart Dictionary of Etymology*, Wilson Co., Bronx NY, 1988, s.v. "fate"

[3] *The Oxford English Dictionary*, Vol. IV, Oxford University Press, NY, 1998 s.v. "fate", Reprinted with permission from The H.W. Wilson Company

[4] *Larousse Encyclopedia of Mythology*, Introduction by Robert Graves, Prometheus Press, NY, 1959, p. 187

[5] *Dictionary of the History of Ideas, Vol. II*, Ed. Phillip Wiener, Charles Scribner's Sons, NY, 1973, p. 226

[6] Wiener, Ed Philipp, *Dictionary of the History of Ideas*, Charles Scribner's Sons, NY, 1973, p. 227

[7] Ibid. pp. 225-236

[8] Ibid.

[9] *Floridan*, February 24, 2002, 10A

[10] Marc Myers, "Lucky You", *Reader's Digest*, October, 2002, pp.166-173

"The proponents of **destiny** have been busy for the last two centuries fostering and developing this word's romanticized appeal."

CHAPTER SIX

Destiny's Deception

Many people believe a force called **destiny** controls human life. Do you have an inevitable **destiny** controlling you? This chapter is going to unravel the empty, twisted logic upon which the concept of **destiny** is based. **Fate** is the grandfather concept from which other "luck theologies" developed. **Destiny, chance**, and **fortune** are all actually descriptive enlargements of the fundamental idea of **fate's** meaning. **Fate**, as we have already studied, expresses a belief in the existence of a god whose power is great enough to control human life. **Destiny** is commonly used by those who believe in a specific declaration by a god-like force, concerning a human life. As with **fate, destiny's** point of reference is the supposed action of a god. Consequently, the meaning of **destiny** projects worthless, idolatrous reasoning and belief. As with **fate**, the meaning of **destiny** stands in direct opposition to the Word of God.

No Such Thing As Luck

> For the Lord *is* great, and greatly to be praised:
> *He* is to be feared [respected] above all gods.
>
> For the gods of the nations *are* idols: but the
> Lord made the heavens.
>
> Psalms 96:4-5

Earlier, we saw devilish deception operating within the concept of **fate**. In this chapter, we are going to see the continuation of that deception operating in **destiny's** concept. Before we get into that deception, we need to look at the background and development of **destiny's** meaning.

What we really have in the development of **destiny's** meaning is the emergence of a lying claim. Clearly, ancient gods were powerless, but the idolaters who bowed down to them said, "They have power." They announced a lying proclamation. They falsely claimed, "The power of the gods we worship is great enough to determine what is going to happen in our lives." This is the sense of meaning for the Latin word, *dëstinãre*. **Destiny's** meaning took root in this Latin word. *Dëstinãre* proclaims the force of action by a god to "fasten down," i.e., to determine a given outcome in a human life; to set its boundaries and to determine its ends.

The definition of **destiny** set forth by *Webster's New World Dictionary* is as follows:

1. The inevitable or necessary succession of events.
2. What will necessarily happen to any person or thing (one's) fortune?
3. That which determines events: said of either a supernatural agency or necessity.
4. [D-], in Greek and Roman Mythology ,The goddess of destiny. The Three Fates – Syn. see Fate. [1]

A brief examination of the above definition will help to reveal **destiny's** close relationship to **fate**. Every essential idea used by *Webster's New World Dictionary* to define **fate** is employed here in its definition for **destiny**. As stated earlier, the key elements in the idea of **fate** were summarized to be: that which is predetermined, declared, and actuated by a god or gods upon human life. This summation fits **destiny** perfectly.

Finally, in *Webster's* fourth sense of this word, we get to the heart of **destiny's** origin - Greek and Roman mythology. Please note that the oldest sense of **destiny** is given last. This is a reversal of the guiding principle that dictionaries normally observe. Here, in the last listed sense of this word, we learn **destiny** is a goddess. The three mystical sisters, earlier called "The Fates," are here called the goddess of **destiny**. The concluding aspect of *Webster's* definition gives **destiny** a synonym. What do you suppose this synonym might be? You are absolutely right; it is the word "**fate**."

In *The Oxford English Dictionary*, there are five senses of **destiny** listed. It is especially noteworthy that "see **Fate**" appears at the end of all five. For example:

> 5. *Mythol*. The goddess of destiny; *pl*. The three goddesses held in Greek and Roman mythology, to determine the course of human life; the Fates: see FATE *sb*. [2]

Destiny, as we are beginning to see, is clearly not distinct from **fate**. These two words are simply different words that describe the same concept. They are words that have the same range of applicability. What can be said of one can be said of the other. They both denote and connote the same idea. Both *fātum* (FATE) and *dëstināre* (DESTINY) refer to the presumed force of a god, to control, and thusly to determine the outcomes of a human life. What we actually have in the concept of both **destiny** and **fate** is the projection of a distorted reality. Both words set forth the lying claim that man-made gods have power. They project the identical absurd meaning.

⌘⌘⌘⌘

Next, we are going to examine the difference in meaning that has developed between **d-e-s-t-i-n-y** and **d-e-s-t-i-n-e**. (In order to fathom the corrupted meaning of **destine** we need to be adventurous enough to tackle a short word study. This will require a little time and two pages worth of patience to get the job done. We need to buckle down and stick with it! It will be a rewarded effort.) *Roget's Thesaurus* gives the following three forms for destiny: verb, adjective, and noun.

Word and meaning	Synonym
Destine *verb* To determine the future of in advance.	FATE *verb*
Destined *adjective* Governed and decided by or as if by fate.	FATED
Destiny *noun* That which is inevitable destined.	FATE *noun*

3

All three forms come directly from the identical root word, *dëstinãre*. Any variation of meaning between these words has to be a corruption of *dëstinãre's* original concept. This is essentially what has happened with the word **destine**. Its present-day meaning is a corruption of *dëstinãre*.

The Oxford English Dictionary's definition of **destiny** is helpful because it shows the weakened variation of meaning between **destiny** and **destine**. *Oxford's* third sense of **destiny** is:

> In weakened sense (cf. DESTINE *v.2*): What in the course of events will become or has become of a person or thing; the ultimate condition. [4]

Today, **destine** refers almost exclusively to an ultimate condition or the end result of what is happening to a person or thing.

It is also important to understand that words such as *designate* and *intend,* have crept into the definition of **destine**. They have changed its emphasis away from controlling gods, and thereby have weakened its original meaning. The usage of these superfluous words is actually a corruption of **destine's** original concept. We need to examine these words briefly.

The word "designate" is derived from the Latin word *designatus,* which means to point out; mark out; indicate; specify. Its basic meaning refers to what, in the course of events, will become of a person or a thing. Designate deals with an ultimate <u>condition</u>, but it does not deal with the actual <u>cause</u> for that condition. (No gods are presumed to be causing the outcome of anything here.) The emphasis for designate is assignment, but it does not name the assignor.

Our word "intend" is derived from the Latin *intendere.* Its basic meaning is to stretch out, or to aim at. Its first sense is purpose or plan. It implies having something in mind. [5] Even though the word "intend" deals with purpose and design, it implies nothing about the cause behind the purpose and design. The actual cause behind the action for this word is not denoted.

By selecting words like designate and intend to define **destine,** we have moved away from a theological context. Remember though, the genuine meaning of **destine** must be defined within its theological context. The original concept for **destine** had no meaning whatsoever, apart from the force of a god controlling the outcome of a human life. This alone is the exclusive origin and meaning for **destine.** Any other meaning has been construed in a later time, and this is exactly what has happened!

In the more modern, corrupt meaning of **destine,** there is little or no reference to a god. For example, look at how *The American Heritage Dictionary* defines **destine:**

1. To determine beforehand; preordain: *a foolish scheme destined to fail; a film destined to become a classic.*
2. To assign for a specific end, use, or purpose: *money destined to pay for their child's education.* [6]

Although theology was originally the main thrust of **destine,** this is no longer true. The modern definition has altogether dropped the theological context.

With the introduction of legitimate terminology that has a <u>similar</u> meaning, the bogus concept of *dëstināre* begins to take on a new legitimacy. By dropping *dëstināre's* theological context, the modern definition for **destine** now has the appearance of a credible meaning. The subtle change of emphasis in the modern definition places the actions of this word upon what is chosen, and away from the chooser (the god). This "slight-of-hand" emphasis change is significant.

Now this word simply refers to an ultimate condition or to the end result of a prior decision. It should be perfectly clear by now, the modern meaning of **destine** is a perversion of *dëstinãre*, and consequently, a corruption of **destiny's** original concept. The original lying claim of **destiny** (the action of a god) now safely hides behind the new, seemingly legitimate idea of **destine** (to designate a purpose or make an assignment). Maybe someone will ask, "What is so significant about all this?"

Destine has become a "trickster" word. Its modern-day meaning shadows and conceals the force responsible for determining the end result. The description of who it is that is responsible for the action in this word remains unnamed, and even masked by obscurity. The one who is operating the "force of determination" is left to the surmising of the individual hearing this word. It is the masked, obscure forces in the modern meaning of **destine** which makes room for the devil to operate his intentions.

Often we hear people make simple statements like: "He is **destined** for greatness," or "She is **destined** for stardom." Well, just WHO is it that has determined the successful outcome for his greatness or her stardom? The force or entity determining their outcomes remains cloaked in obscurity. It is not named. Do you care to guess what that force might be? Actually, there is no need to guess. The implication is abundantly clear. It is that "great power of determination" we saw in the last chapter popping up again.

No Such Thing As Luck

When the May 14-16, 2004 "USA Weekend" magazine article, (Who's News), reports that Oprah Winfrey said, "She realized why she never had children: she was **destined** to care for neglected or needy kids." What does the phrase "she was **destined**" suppose to mean? Who was responsible for the decision to care for neglected and needy kids? The implied meaning of **destined** is clear. Some mysterious, supernatural power was at work, determining the outcome for her.

The fictitious power of **fate** is now called by its updated name - **destiny**; and the meaning of **destiny** is concealed behind the respectable appearance and cleverly disguised modern definition of **destine**. When the phony concept of **fate** gets exposed for the "laughing-stock" that it is, its new name **destiny** appears. When the ridiculous concept of **destiny** gets exposed for the "laughing-stock" that it is, the mask of obscurity worn by the word **destine** pops up to continue **destiny's** deception. The original devilish deception of **fate** was that idolatrous gods have the power to control human life. The deception of **destiny** only projects a new name for the same lie, and the modern-day concept of **destine** has provided a means to continue the original deception of **destiny's** meaning. The implied meaning of "it was meant to be" or "**destined** to be" needs honest confrontation. When the implied power in the meaning of **destine** is fully named, then we are able to grasp its deviant idolatrous meaning.

⌘⌘⌘⌘

The modern day usage of the word **destiny** has another aspect that needs to be understood. The proponents of **destiny** have been busy for the last two centuries, fostering and developing this word's romanticized appeal. Sadly, they have succeeded. Romantics have successfully elevated the concept of **destiny** by making it attractive, appealing and inviting. Consequently, the word has been given an elevated sense of glory. The Romantics in literature, theater, politics and other fields have used the concept of **destiny** to foster their ideals and to justify their purposes. For example: "manifest destiny" became a popular term used by politicians to justify the U. S. Government's accumulating Western Territories in the mid 1800's.

Today, the romanticized idea of **destiny** remains popular. Typing in the word **destiny** on the Google internet search engine brought up 3,100,000 web-site listings. The glamour and appeal of this word has led thousands of business owners to include **destiny** in their company's name. Destiny Insurance Company, Radio Destiny Network, Digital Destiny Inc., Destiny Products Inc., *Challenging Destiny* Magazine, Wings of Destiny (a promotion agency), and Destiny Hearts (a dating club) are just a few examples; but the list goes on and on. These business owners know the appeal and magnetism of this word.

In its romantic context, **destiny** is usually projected to be a force that brings about an appealing, good result. This aspect of **destiny**'s concept has been made suggestive, imaginative, and even flirtatious. This is what gives it its romantic appeal. For example, if in the face of all obstacles, one finds that marriage partner with whom they are well pleased, they might give the credit to **destiny**. Many newlyweds glory in **destiny**'s having brought them together in marriage (though they might not say so later on).

No Such Thing As Luck

Romantic **destiny** could be described as the getting of help from a larger, outside source, which brings an almost impossible, victorious achievement to one's life. This victorious accomplishment is often attributed to the work of **destiny**. There is absolutely no basis in fact for such a strange conclusion; however, the romantic idea of **destiny** uses fanciful illogical explanations to explain events.

The romantic proponents of **destiny** rise up and proclaim, "My having received a victorious accomplishment over every obstacle is a sign, even a proof, of **destiny**'s blessing. How favored I am because **destiny** has smiled upon me. **Destiny** has lifted me up over every obstacle and has given me this victory." This is what people often say about its romantically appealing notion, "It just has to be **destiny** - what else could it be?" In their confused minds, **destiny** is the source that elevates individuals and provides great, outstanding accomplishments. If they are going to have great success, success will come because **destiny** acts upon their lives. This is the way they think, and their distorted reasoning makes **destiny** their provider, their rewarder, and even their god.

⌘⌘⌘⌘

Destiny has no power. It cannot proclaim its own works. Someone must stand up on its behalf and voice its lying claims. In reality, **destiny** is nothing more than a lofty personification of attractive, but worthless words. Its appealing ideas are designed to hook and to snare the innocent. Here are a few of the enticing lies propounded by the disciples of **destiny**:

"Destiny shows favoritism; it rewards individuals even though they have done nothing to receive its favor."
"Destiny pays no attention to morality; it elevates both the good and the bad."
"Destiny calls to greatness. It chooses individuals for great purposes."
"Destiny calls, it calls individuals, but it also calls nations."
"Destiny is an active force, maneuvering minute human affairs and circumstances, acting unexpectantly."
"Destiny cannot be summoned nor can it be appeased. It determines what is 'meant to be'."
"Destiny dashes into pieces the best efforts and high ambitions of men."

It is perfectly obvious that the proponents of **destiny** are seeking to deceive. By their words of intrigue, people are entrapped. By the constant use of this concept, people become attracted to its familiar idea. The dazzle and appeal of romanticized, whimsical words dupe people into believing outlandish lies. The fundamental lie embraced within the concept of **destiny** is that the individual's efforts, energies, and disciplines are not the controlling power in life. The highest controlling power remains that unseen force out there; it is the ultimate cause bringing a blessing or a cursing – it's **destiny**.

⌘⌘⌘⌘

No Such Thing As Luck

What a sad day this would be if all this were true! But, it is NOT true. Individual efforts, energies, and disciplines are the true causes for most all of our accomplishments in life. Additionally, the Christian Believer can look beyond any of his personal limitations. He can operate the power that God has given him, which makes him sufficient for any circumstance. He is in command of his own life.

> I can do all things through Christ which strengtheneth me.
>   Philippians 4:13

Why would any sound-minded man or woman be taken in by **destiny**'s romantic appeal? They would not! Why would any spiritually minded, conscientious man or woman ever look to the supposed power of **destiny,** or any other false, glittering, alluring power to bring good upon their lives? They would not! **Destiny** is both a downer and a loser. To believe in its precepts is a "dead-end-street", leading to disappointment and despair.

Christian Believers must always look to their Heavenly Father. He alone is the true and authentic supplier of peace and prosperity. We can cast all our cares upon Him, for He cares for us. He heals all our diseases. He makes us whole. His love is real. We can depend upon His power to lift us up and to set us on the high places in life. He is our sure reward.

⌘⌘⌘⌘

The Bible does use the word "predestinate", and we need to consider this word in our study of **destiny**. As we shall see, the biblical usage of predestinate is vastly different from the pagan concept of **destiny**. Any valid discussion about predestinate must take into consideration the "predestinator."

> According as He [God] hath chosen us in Him before the foundation of the world, that we should be holy and without blame before Him in love:
>
> Having predestinated us unto the adoption [sonship] of children by Jesus Christ to Himself, according to the good pleasure of His will.
>
> Ephesians 1:4-5

Because God is all knowing, His view of eternity perceives the beginning and the end. His foreknowledge precedes our choices. He does not determine our choices; however, he knows, in advance, what we will choose.

> Thus, in God's omniscience, the past, the present, and the future are all equal realities. God sees the future as though it were happening in the present. But God does not necessarily directly *cause* the event of the future to take place. God will never overstep man's free will; rather, looking ahead He can see what choice will be made and therefore pronounce that it will be so. Thus, God's foreknowledge precedes predestination. [7]

No Such Thing As Luck

This is how we are predestinated to become children of God, born of God's spirit.

God knew beforehand that we would choose to believe that He raised His Son, Jesus Christ, from the dead. He knew beforehand that we would choose to make Jesus Christ the Lord of our lives. God knew we would be born again of His spirit. Although God's will is that everyone be born again of His spirit; not everyone will choose to believe God raised Jesus Christ from the dead. God will never force His will upon anyone. We do the choosing; we choose to believe God and His Wonderful Word, or else we choose to loose.

⌘⌘⌘⌘

The outstanding problem people have with the word "predestinate" comes from mistakenly associating it with the concept of **destiny**. Within the concept of **destiny**, "a god" always does the choosing, and then casts his decision upon a human life. The word "predestinate" is used four times in the Bible, and it never refers to God's determining anything apart from our ability to choose.

God would never cast anything upon us that would negate our ability to choose. God knows the future. He knew ahead of time the choices we would make in our lives. He knew that we would believe in the resurrection of Jesus Christ from the dead. God knew we would decide to make Jesus Christ the Lord of our lives, God knew we would react to His Word in just this manner, that we would become sons of God, born of His spirit.

That if thou shalt confess with thy mouth the
Lord Jesus [make Jesus the lord of your life]
and shalt believe in thine heart that God hath
raised him from the dead, thou shalt be saved.

For with the heart man believeth unto
righteousness; and with the mouth confession
is made unto salvation.

Romans 10:9-10

⌘⌘⌘⌘

Sadly, countless numbers of people embrace the
outlandish doctrines of **destiny** today. Consequently, they
remain in darkness. They lack realistic proof to substantiate
their misguided beliefs and confessions. What they have
chosen to believe about **destiny** stands in direct opposition
to God and His Word. The "destiny seekers" of our day are
no different from those who are described in the biblical
record of 1 Kings, Chapter Eighteen.

The nation of Israel was desolate when King Ahab reigned.
Israel was in the midst of a drought because they were
worshipping Baal (their god of **destiny**). Then, the prophet
Elijah had Ahab gather that entire idolatrous nation to Mount
Carmel for a showdown with their false prophets.

And Elijah came unto all the people, and said,
How long halt ye between two opinions? If
the Lord *be* God, follow Him: but if Baal, *then*

> follow him. And the people answered him not
> a word.
>
> 1 Kings 18:21

The people of this nation were going to judge between the power of God and the power of Baal.

> And call ye on the name of your gods, and I
> will call on the name of the Lord: and the God
> that answereth by fire, let him be God. And
> all the people answered and said, It is well
> spoken.
>
> 1 Kings 18:24

Early that morning the prophets of Baal prepared and presented their sacrifices. These false prophets were given every opportunity to demonstrate the power of their god before the eyes of Israel. They called upon Baal throughout the entire day. They pleaded and they prophesied. They cried aloud, boisterously. They even cut themselves with knives till the blood ran out of their bodies – a proof of their sincerity and their passion.

The eyes of that nation looked all day upon the unanswered prayers and pleadings offered to their false god of **destiny**. Baal was now exposed; he was powerless to answer. He was a fake, powerless god. So, Israel's false god had now been exposed before their very faces! Now what?

After all the activity of this day, at the set time of the evening offering, Elijah prepared an altar and placed a sacrifice upon it. Then he prayed this simple prayer:

> Lord God of Abraham, Isaac, and of Israel, let
> it be known this day that Thou *art* God in Israel,
> and *that* I *am* Thy servant, and *that* I have done
> all these things at Thy word.
>
> Hear me, O Lord, hear me, that this people
> may know that Thou *art* the Lord God, and
> *that* Thou hast turned their heart back again.
>
> 1 Kings 18:36b-37

The day was drawing to a close, but the people of Israel continued to watch. They were about to witness a vast contrast between their powerless god of **destiny** and the undeniable great manifestation of the True God's power. The reality of God's presence and power would persuade them and change their lives. His answer was by fire!

> Then the fire of the Lord fell, and consumed
> the burnt sacrifice, and the wood, and the
> stones, and the dust, and licked up the water
> that *was* in the trench.
>
> And when all the people saw *it*, they fell on
> their faces: and they said, The Lord, He *is* the
> God; the Lord, He *is* the God.
>
> 1 Kings 18:38-39

People today just need to make up their minds; which God are they going to serve? They need to become persuaded about the True and Living God and the truth of His Word. To rely upon the false power of **destiny,** and to depend upon it, is to call upon a lifeless, idolatrous god. **Destiny** is only a deception, but to love God and trust His Word, makes a sure foundation for any man, woman, boy, or girl.

135

Delight thyself also in the Lord; and He shall
give thee the desires of thine heart.

Psalm 37:4

---

[1] *Webster's New World Dictionary*, World Pub., N.Y., 1968, s.v. "destiny"

[2] *The Oxford English Dictionary*, Volume IV, Second Edition, Oxford, Oxford University Press, 2001, s.v. "destiny"

[3] *Roget's II The New Thesaurus, Expanded Edition*, Houghton Mifflin Company, Boston, Mass., 1988, p. 269

[4] *The Oxford English Dictionary*, Volume IV, s.v. "destiny"

[5] *Webster's New World Dictionary*, s.v. "intend"

[6] *The American Heritage Dictionary*, Third Edition, Houghton Mifflin Co., Boston, 1992, s.v. "destine"

[7] Wierwille, V.P., *Jesus Christ Our Passover*, American Christian Press, New Knoxville, OH, 1980, p. 464

"Pagan idolatry, magical illusions, animated objects, and the self-proclaimed 'gifted ability' to interpret a message from a fake god all form the framework for the ancient concept of **lots**."

CHAPTER SEVEN

A Little About A Lot

In the previous chapter, we learned that the popular notion of **destiny** is that which is declared by a god, and its meaning is clearly not distinct from **fate**. How does the word **lot** relate to the concept of **fate**? **Lot** is the <u>method</u> for understanding what **fate** has to say.

The ancient use of lot casting is vastly different from its modern secular use, or is it? Most all of us are familiar with the present day secular usage for the word **lot**, for example:

1. The choice resulting from the casting of lots.
2. A portion or a share that is assigned by lots.
3. The amount due as in a tax.
4. A plot or portion of land.
5. A considerable number, quantity. [1]

No Such Thing As Luck

There are other secular definitions for this word, but without exception, all these secular concepts have moved away from lot's original theological sense. Modern day meanings of lot generally exclude the religious sense of the word. Just as the meaning of **destiny** was weakened, the true meaning of lot has decayed. It has decayed into secular terminology, far removed from its first intended theological meaning. Originally, its meaning was the method of obtaining a message from a god.

Today, we generally use the word **lot** in reference to the action of casting objects such as dice, or drawing numbered objects to obtain a decision believed to have been caused by **chance**. We will be looking at the word **chance** in more detail later. But for now, we need to see how the ridiculous idea of **chance** has become a substitute, replacing the idea of a god's action, or power. As such, **chance** is a cover-up word. It is used to cover-up the idolatrous acknowledgement that ascribes power to a supposed god. The word **chance** is an abstract and dubious term, but it has become more acceptable than the ancient meaning of **lot**. It is more acceptable today because it replaces the concept of idolatrous gods hovering around us, and controlling decisions about our lives. People today mistakenly think in terms of leaving things up to **chance**.

We are fundamentally interested in how and why the concept of **lot** fits into the dictionary definition of **luck**. Therefore, we are going to restrict our study of **lot** generally to its theological aspects. As we are about to see, *The Oxford Dictionary* includes both ancient and modern senses for this word.

Lot

1. Any of a set of objects used in a method of random selection to secure a decision in deciding disputes, dividing goods, choosing people for an office or duty, etc., by an appeal to chance or the divine agency supposed to be concerned in the results of chance.
2. The action or an act of casting, drawing, etc. lots, to obtain a decision.
3. A portion, a share; *spec.* what is assigned by lot as a person's share or portion in an inheritance or a distribution of property; a division or share of property made by lot.
4. What is given to a person by fate or divine providence; *esp.* a person's destiny, fortune, or condition in life. [2]

The central theme in the above definition is a religious process for securing information. The action in the word **lot** is clearly that of casting forth lots to secure a message from a super-natural entity. The super-natural entity, a god, is thought to direct the procedure and to reveal its will. This is the sense and meaning of the word **lot** in history, and especially in its inception. There can be no mistake about it. The ancient concept of **lot** casting centered on idolatrous belief in the power of pagan gods. **Lot** casting was an activity that required a confession of belief and expectation in the ability of a god to manifest its decrees.

No Such Thing As Luck

⌘⌘⌘⌘

The central issue with which we are concerned in our study of the **lot** is between divination and revelation. After studying the deceitful practice of divination, we will consider the function of receiving truthful revelation. Divination is a human device that employs magical arts as a means of seeking special knowledge from a god.

> The underlying thought in all forms of divination is that by employing certain means, men are able to obtain knowledge otherwise beyond their reach. [3]

The practice of divination has always been mistakenly predicated upon the factual existence of a god's power to answer.

Since the gods of history were powerless to speak, the priesthood surrounding pagan deities spoke on their behalf. They utilized bones, sticks, unusual rocks, and other objects to magically divine a message. The gods had no power to answer, but the priesthood, representing false idols, by deception and trickery, determined what was believed to be the god's response. Priests would gaze upon the pattern of the "magical" object they had cast before their idols. Then they would interpret what they claimed was a message from their god. In reality, the message was, of course, the priests' message. The priest could give any interpretation he chose and then deceitfully declare his own message to be from the gods he represented. Pagan priests were masters of illusion. People were hoodwinked and lured into accepting the validity of what the priests declared. Individuals, and even entire nations, were tricked into believing the priests' messages were actually from the deities they called upon.

On the occasion of Jehoshaphat the king of Judah visiting Ahab, king of Israel, both kings were deceived into entering a war with Syria by lying prophets and priests. The lying prophets of Baal claimed the special insight to know the ensuing battle's outcome; they served Baal but on this occasion presumed to speak for Jehovah God.

> And the king of Israel and Jehoshaphat the king of Judah sat each on his throne, having put on their robes, in a void place in the entrance of the gate of Samaria; and all the prophets prophesied before them.
>
> And Zedekiah the son of Chenaanah made him horns of iron: and he said, Thus saith the Lord, With these shalt thou push the Syrians, until thou have consumed them.
>
> And all the prophets prophesied so, saying, Go up to Ramothgilead, and prosper: for the Lord shall deliver *it* into the king's hand.
>
> 1 Kings 22:10-12

Both kings believed the deceptive prophecy and went up to battle with the Syrians, but to their demise. Jehoshophat barely escaped the battle with his life. Ahab did not escape; a Syrian arrow mortally wounded him. In this particular record, the lying priesthood that successfully lured these nations into war was itself deceived by devil spirit revelation and possession.

Mystical experiences have been a vital part of man-made religion. Idol worship would have lost its appeal without a mystical nature. Mysticism gave a seeming power to powerless gods. The appeal for worshipping false idols was built upon this "seeming power"; the power of a god seemed to exist. The mystical side of pagan religion also gave significant importance to feelings and emotions. Shaded, dark understandings and nuances of meaning were key elements built into religious rituals. Deceiving practices that could enhance the "appearance" of a supposed supernatural power were commonly used to fool and beguile the innocent. Something about idols and gods had to give a showy appearance of power. The priesthood had to make lifeless gods give this "seeming appearance of life." All of this was designed to provoke people's belief, and confidence.

The average person on the street lacked the ability to divine answers from their gods. This is where the priest and the visionary found job security for themselves. They claimed an "inborn gift" - that special ability required to successfully represent a particular god (to perceive the spiritual and see beyond the physical). Their claims of special perception and magical insight lured people to worship at their altars.[4] Clairvoyant priests were respected and even revered. They could manipulate the **lot**; they could utilize psychic vision; they could interpret so called **chance** happenings; they could explain the coincidental. They would do whatever it took to give the appearance of communicating with their gods. The main stay of their activity centered on their ability to receive information from a presumed higher power. They were called "priests" but they were more than simple priests. They were magicians, astrologers, sorcerers, charmers and wizards, enchanters, diviners, and they were consulters of evil spirits. They were in fact "false priests."

The aura around pagan temples and pagan gods gave a magical appearance. The design and décor of idolatrous temples were built to impress with the greatest pomp, splendor, and mystique. For example, the Babylonian temple built for Murduk equaled the height of a modern thirty-story skyscraper. Once the worshipper ascended all the plateaus and stairways leading to the top of this gigantic temple, the image of Murduk was there to behold. The ancient historian Herodotus established the weight of this idol at over twenty-six tons, and it was supposedly constructed of pure gold. [5]

People were dazzled and deceived by the theater, the dramatics, and the ritualistic show. When the priests of Murduk cast down their magical **lot**, the authority of their interpretation was almost unquestionable. The enormous splendor of a temple and the renown of the god whom they represented backed up their prestige, position, and importance. All of these mystical surroundings, the dream-world beauty, the charming exuberance, the impressiveness, and especially the international renown of Murduk, belonged to the care and keeping of priests. These pagan priests were arrogant boasters, and masters of illusion, to whom vast numbers of simple people paid homage, respect, and awe.

The **lot** was an invaluable means of divination for a pagan priest. This was the means by which he demonstrated his special expertise to obtain secret knowledge. His skillful ability to successfully cast a set of animated objects (lots) was the trademark of his authority. His self-proclaimed "gifted insight", supposedly enabled him to both read and interpret the diversity of arrangements obtained in the casting forth of his potent objects. It is important for us to understand, however, that the message conveyed by the **lot** was always projected to be both the words and work of a god.

Essentially, the **lot** was viewed to be a means and a method by which a god could reveal his will. The message was always the important thing. What does this god have to say about my life? The "itching ears" of an idolatrous worshipper wanted desperately to know what a god had determined for his life. He believed that by the priest's magical **lot** he could get the answers he sought. The priest knew that as long as he could manipulate his magical **lot,** he could maintain control over the lives of those who worshipped at the altar of the god he represented.

This is the idolatrous context from which our word **lot** developed. And, what a sordid context it is! Pagan idolatry, magical illusions, animated objects, and the self-proclaimed "gifted ability" to interpret a message from a fake god, all form the framework for the ancient concept of **lots**. There is simply nothing about the fallacious concept of pagan **lot** casting that deserves legitimate recognition. To the contrary, the concept of the **lot** of divination is pagan "hogwash" and natural-minded stupidity. The Levitical Law strictly forbade its use.

There shall not be found among you *any one* that make his son or his daughter to pass through the fire [of Moloch], *or* that useth divination, *or* an observer of times, or an enchanter, or a witch.

Deuteronomy 18:10

⌘⌘⌘⌘

Eventually, with the passing of time, the concept of **lot** casting came to stand for determination itself. Today, our dictionaries present **lot** with this sense of meaning. The **lot** is now more readily understood to mean that which is determined in a random selection by an appeal to **chance**. There is no problem with this, as long as we define **chance** to mean something beyond our knowledge and control. There is a huge problem, however, when **chance** becomes a substitute term that stands for the work of an unseen god.

When individuals submit to the controlling concept of "my **lot** in life," they are practicing a modern-day form of idolatry. They are confessing to spiritual possession. The essential difference between the ancient and modern-day idol-worshipper is easy to understand. The ancient idolater openly bowed down before the images he worshipped. The modern day idolater sheepishly bows in his heart. He accepts and embraces "chance theologies." He embraces the force of **luck**. He believes in the power of **fate** and **destiny**; he willingly accepts his **lot**.

Often today, we hear submissive confessions like the following: "My **lot** in life is so and so," or "My **lot** has fallen out to be this or that." These revealing statements are very

147

suggestive. Individuals making these loaded statements are really proclaiming that some force greater than themselves (that great unseen "force of determination") is at work controlling what is happening to them. This is their confession of belief. Those who thoughtlessly and carelessly embrace this kind of logic need to stop it immediately. Idolatrous logic always gets people "in hot water." God dealt with the practice of idolatry extensively in the book of Jeremiah. The following is a tremendous description of an idolatrous man.

> Every man is brutish in *his* knowledge: every founder is confounded by the graven image: for his molten image *is* falsehood, and *there* is no breath in them.
>
> They *are* vanity, *and* the work of errors: in the time of their visitation they shall perish.
>
> Jeremiah 10:14-15

Those who bow in their thinking, and vainly try to legitimize the supposed forces behind the concepts of **lot**, **destiny**, and **fate**, are engaging in worthless vanity. God's Word abounds with examples that show the fruitlessness of idolatrous practices. The Old Testament nations of Judah and Israel were removed from their promised land inheritance because of their idolatrous beliefs and practices. Disappointment, despair, and defeat have always followed hard upon the lives of those who worship worthless, false images.

⌘⌘⌘⌘

We have before us here a vivid contrast that needs to be seen for what it is. The man-made pseudo religion we have been looking at, stands in opposition to the powerful and uplifting relationship Christian Believers should and must have with our Heavenly Father. Christian Believers have never needed a mysterious casting of the **lot** to receive a message from God. We have the genuine revelation of God's Word, the Bible. The message of God's Word is clear and simple. Eighty to eighty-five percent of the Bible needs no interpretation; the message is perfectly clear and understandable, just as it is written. The remaining difficult verses need study, and we are urged in the Bible to do so.

> Study to shew thyself approved unto God, a workman that needeth not to be ashamed, rightly dividing the word of truth.
> 2 Timothy 2:15

We are to be students and workmen of God's Word, because God's Word is The Word of Truth. It is not some man-made philosophy, or story, or doctrine about a supposed god that only reveals his will to certain magical priests by the casting of a **lot**. God's Word can be trusted because it is a Faithful Word. It is a Sure Word. What God promises in His Word He always brings to pass; He performs even the smallest details. God's Word is a personal word, and it is addressed to all that will believe it.

> For this cause also thank we God without ceasing, because, when ye received the word of God which ye heard of us, ye received it not as the word of men, but as it is in truth, the word of God, which effectually [powerfully] worketh also in you that believe.
>
> 1 Thessalonians 2:13

The empty, anemic words spoken by false priests and prophets fell to the ground because they were vain and worthless words. God's Word is a Powerful Word. It is dynamic in its message and in its content. It deals with every essential issue of life and eternity.

> According as His divine power hath given unto us all things that *pertain* unto life and godliness, through the knowledge of Him that hath called us to glory and virtue:
>
> 2 Peter 1:3

The relationship we have with our God is such that we can walk and talk with Him on a daily basis. We, who are born again of God's spirit, have the ability to walk in the glorious power and authority He has given us. By our operation of discerning of spirits we can cast out devil spirits. We have the ability to minister healing to the sick. We can speak with new tongues. By our God-given ability, we can literally speak forth a message from God to bless our fellowship of Christian Believers. God teaches us via the spirit He has given us; and by this spirit we have a direct link with Him. The tremendous benefits of speaking in tongues belong to us! We can praise God perfectly; we can maintain restful minds; and, we can build ourselves up spiritually, with might in our inner man. We strengthen our lives inwardly as we operate speaking in tongues in our private prayer life.

The imperative need is for Christian Believers to walk and live life, openly demonstrating the power of their God-given abilities. We must walk in that power and with that efficacy. For us there is never a need for a magical casting of **lots**. There is no need for a mystical priesthood. We communicate with God on our own behalf. God's method is to communicate with the individual personally and directly. By our operation of word of wisdom, word of knowledge, and discerning of spirits, God teaches us. He teaches us the necessary information and the required action to bring about His deliverance for our lives and the lives of His people. God does fortify His message to the individual from time to time, by sending prophets and others to establish His Word, but He deals with the individual first and foremost. We hear directly from God by receiving His written word, and by the personal information He reveals to us from day to day.

⌘⌘⌘⌘

As interesting and informative as it would be, the scope of our study will not allow us to treat all the usages of **lot** casting utilized in the Bible. However, before closing this chapter we need to look briefly at the use of the Urim and Thummin. God did, on numerous occasions, answer individuals with specific information by means of two special stones named the Urim and Thummin. These stones were retrieved from a pouch constructed in the breastplate of the ephod worn by the High Priest of Israel. The High Priest's presence and authority was required to receive an answer from God concerning a specific inquiry by Israel or by an individual. God did ordain the use of this method of prayer and inquiry for Old Testament believers who lived under the Levitical Law. One occasion of its use is given in the book of First Samuel. David employed this special method of inquiry after the Amalekites had invaded his small city, named Ziklag. They had burnt Ziklag and taken captive his family and all his belongings. Before this disaster, David had been on the downside in his relationship with God, but on this occasion, he restored that broken fellowship by encouraging himself in the Lord his God.

> And David said to Abiathar the [high] priest, Ahimelech's son, I pray thee, bring me hither the ephod. And Abiathar brought thither the ephod to David.

> And David inquired at the Lord, saying, Shall I pursue after this troop? Shall I overtake them? And he answered him, Pursue: for thou shalt overtake *them*, and without fail recover *all*.
> 1 Samuel 30:7-8

The message David received was to pursue the Amalekites, and he would recover ALL! This is exactly what came to pass.

> And David recovered all that the Amalekites had carried away: and David rescued his two wives.

And there was nothing lacking to them, neither
small nor great, neither sons nor daughters,
neither spoil, nor any thing that they had taken
to them: David recovered all.

1 Samuel 30:18-19

There is a vast difference between the biblical Urim and
Thummin and the counterfeit **lot** cast by pagan priests. When
God answered the High Priest of Israel by this method, the
answer was authentic; it was a true message from God and it
came to pass. When pagan priests cast their **lots** before dumb
idols, the answers were false. Their answers were lies, because
they were answers conjured up by the pagan priests
themselves. False gods cannot speak so they have no answers.
The pagan priests' answers were vain and worthless. All along,
throughout history, false prophets and priests have spoken
deceitfully about their gods. They have even been bold
enough to stand up and speak lies and half-truths,
presumptuously claiming to represent the true and eternal
God of heaven and earth. Divination is a corruption of true
prophecy. God's answer has always been with power and
authority. When He had a message to proclaim by a prophet,
that which was proclaimed always came to pass.

But the prophet, which shall presume to speak
a word in My name, which I have not
commanded him to speak, or that shall speak
in the name of other gods, even that prophet
shall die.

And if thou say in thine heart, How shall we
know the word which the Lord hath not
spoken?

No Such Thing As Luck

> When a prophet speaketh in the name of the Lord, if the thing follow not, nor come to pass, that is the thing which the Lord hath not spoken, but the prophet hath spoken it presumptuously: thou shalt not be afraid of him.
>
> Deuteronomy 18:20-22

⌘⌘⌘⌘

Now that we have examined the pagan belief and practice associated with the word **lot,** we are in a better position to question the validity of this word's meaning. The original concept of the heathen **lot** projects the worthless, vain images of idolatrous belief. The word's meaning is absurd. Nevertheless, its meaning and acceptance continues in our day and time.

The long-standing concept of **lot** makes it an apt choice of words in defining **luck**. Most any dictionary's effort to define **luck** will employ the word **lot** because it fits so comfortably. The old adage about "birds of a feather sticking together" is certainly true of **lot** and **luck**. These two words are more than distant cousins. **Lot** and **luck** are sisters; they come from the identical, idolatrous family. Now that the illegitimate operation of **lot's** meaning has been plainly set before us, we can dispose of its value. Any credibility it may have had in our thinking is over and gone. Once people begin to realize the absurdity of this fictitious, ancient concept, they have no problem dismissing its use. **Lot's** worthless meaning for defining **luck** stands condemned.

154

[1] *Oxford Dictionary of the English Language*, Oxford, Oxford University Press, 1999, s.v. "lot"

[2] *Ibid.*

[3] *The International Standard Bible Encyclopedia*, Wm. B. Eerdmans Pub. Co., Grand Rapids, MI, 1960, article by T. Witton Davis, s.v. "divination"

[4] Gulley, Rosemary E., *Harpers Encyclopedia of Mystical and Paranormal Experience*, Castle Books, NY, NY, 1991, pp. 384-385

[5] Ceram, C.W., *Gods, Graves, and Scholars*, Alfred A. Knopf, Inc., NY, 1967, pp. 289-292

"The utilization of **fortune**, as it is defined currently, continues to elevate and legitimize the identical power that was traditionally associated with the goddess Fortuna."

CHAPTER EIGHT

Fortune's Fallacy

Many people believe the happy life is the **fortunate** life. **Fortune,** they claim, is a distinct help in human affairs. They say it brings success to our lives - the expected variety, and the unexpected variety also. They say that although **fortune** shocks us with unexpected behavior and irrationality, it controls the power of wealth, riches, prosperity, and renown. Have you ever been blessed by good **fortune?** Is **fortune** truly a legitimate entity with the ability to bestow benefits upon whomever it chooses? Who is the ultimate bestower of blessings? This is what we need to know.

The controversy which surrounds **luck** is blatantly portrayed in the concept of **fortune.** What has been taught about the concept of **fortune** helps to fortify teachings about **luck.** Consequently, our modern day ideas about **luck** rest comfortably upon the foundation that **fortune** has provided. **Fortune** is **luck's** older sister. Actually, **luck** gains its presumed legitimacy from what has been taught and believed for centuries about the idea of **fortune**.

The concept of **fortune** is no less illegitimate than the other concepts we have studied. Its origin is goddess worship. The idolatrous religions that produced empty beliefs regarding **fate** and **destiny** also produced the worthless concept of **fortune**. **Fortune** is usually viewed to be the favorable decision of some unknown force to bestow good. Its fundamental meaning, however, projects the unsound conclusions of an idolatrous mind-set. But, ancient beliefs about the concept of **fortune** continue to influence our present day logic and beliefs. Because of this injurious influence, we need to unravel **fortune's** twisted meaning.

⌘⌘⌘⌘

In order to understand our Modern English word **fortune**, we must first understand a few essential aspects of Fortuna, the Roman goddess. Beliefs and rituals that were centered around this goddess ultimately produced today's meaning of **fortune**. We dealt with the goddess Fortuna in an earlier chapter. She was worshipped extensively throughout the Roman Empire. Plinty the Elder of first century Rome gives the following description of how widespread Fortuna worship became:

> Everywhere in the whole world at every hour by all men's voices fortune [Fortuna] alone is invoked and named, alone accused, alone

impeached, alone pondered, alone applauded, alone rebuked and visited with reproaches; deemed volatile and indeed by most men blind as well, wayward, inconstant, uncertain, fickle in her favors and favoring the unworthy. To her is debited all that is spent and credited, all that is received, she alone fills both pages in the whole of mortals' account; [1]

The intricate details of Fortuna worship are not essential to our study. What we do know about her accents the good benefits she could supposedly deliver, or bestow, upon those who worshipped at her feet.

According to the authorities, therefore, the worship of Fortuna was not a surrender to chance or randomness in which individual effort was abandoned; it was much more an attempt to propitiate the goddess so that she would smile on an undertaking. Fortuna may be capricious but her behavior is not random. [2]

So then, she was worshipped primarily for benefits, but her gifts were rewarded according to her whims and discretion. The aspect of uncertainty may have been associated with her character, but it was not a focal point. The focal point of her appeal centered upon what the Romans believed was her power to deliver a benefit. There were many gods and goddesses that were believed to "dole out" doom, but not Fortuna. She was not feared; rather she was sought for her blessings. To seek the acclaimed favor of this goddess was believed to be a legitimate means of achieving success.

No Such Thing As Luck

The *New Larousse Encyclopedia of Mythology* gives the following description of Fortuna:

> A golden statuette of Fortuna had always to remain in the sleeping quarters of Roman Emperors. Citizens who were distinguished by outstanding good or bad luck had a Fortuna. When overtaken at sea by a storm, Caesar said to the terrified pilot: "What do you fear? You carry Caesar and his Fortuna."
>
> The countless representations of Fortuna show her chief attributes to be the wheel, the sphere, a ship's rudder and prow, and a cornucopia. [3]

Fortuna's influence continues to live among us today. The wheel-of-fortune can be traced directly to her imagery. Her ship's rudder is suggestive of her supposed ability to direct the affairs of men. The cornucopia represents her bold claim to be a goddess of bountiful supply. The common modern-day terminology that describes the concept of **luck**, in the feminine gender, emanates directly from Fortuna. **Luck** became "Lady Luck" because of its close association with this Roman goddess.

⌘⌘⌘⌘

There is no problem tracing our word **fortune** straight back to the goddess, Fortuna. The *Barnhart Dictionary of Etymology* shows the development of Fortuna's name.

... Latin *fortûna*, from a lost noun **fortus* (genitive **fortûs*), from *fors* (genitive *fortis*) chance, luck, possibly (as being what is brought) related to *ferre* carry, [4]

The Latin word, *fors,* emphasizes what is brought forth or delivered, and Fortuna was the goddess who brought it forth. The basic meaning here is not the modern concept of **chance.**

Chance today implies without a cause. The fundamental meaning in **fortune's** etymology is the deliberate bringing forth of success, and this success was originally attributed to the widely acclaimed power named Fortuna. The renowned qualities and attributes of this goddess form the basis upon which our word, **fortune,** is construed. Our modern concept of **fortune** actually keeps the sordid theological beliefs that surrounded Fortuna alive and active.

As we are about to see, our current dictionary's explanation of **fortune** describes this very process - the process by which a supposed supernatural force grants something to an individual. The following definition of **fortune** also continues the same theological theme we saw earlier in the words, **fate, destiny,** and **lot.** All these words, as we already know, are subjects of theology. Our word **fortune** plainly developed from a pagan religious setting. *Webster's New World Dictionary's* definition is:

Fortune [ME,; OFr.; L. *fortuna,* chance, hap, fate, fortune...]

1. the supposed power considered to bring good or bad to people; luck; chance; fate; often personified. [5]

No Such Thing As Luck

Notice that *Webster's* definition makes a reference to a "supposed power." However, this definition does not say who this supposed power is; nor does it go out of the way to name the "supposers." In reference to these "supposers," *Webster's* says they "considered" this unnamed power to bring good or bad to people. What *Webster's* should have actually said, is that they literally "believe in" **fortune's** power to bring good. In fact, *Webster's* unnamed "supposers" do believe in a certain, supernatural power called **fortune**, but in Roman history, this power was called Fortuna!

Webster's failure to name this power, and those who believed in it, is a lost opportunity. The editors of *Webster's New World Dictionary*, assuredly, knew both the name of the supposed power, and the identity of those who professed a belief in it. In their word derivative of **fortune**, they show the following:

ME.; OFr.; L. *fortuna*

Only two word entries away, the name Fortuna is defined. There, the definition of Fortuna is simply: "in *Roman Mythology*, the goddess of fortune." [6] Beyond question, the editors of this dictionary knew this "supposed power" to be the goddess Fortuna. It is also clear they knew it was Roman Mythology that helped to produce this goddess. Their cautious effort has failed to properly define a fictitious pagan concept in straightforward, legitimate language. They could have been much more forthcoming in their attempt to define its meaning. They could have defined **fortune** to be: the modern term that reflects the misguided and superstitious belief of ancient Romans, who worshipped a false goddess named Fortuna - Romans who mistakenly attributed to Fortuna the power to bring good benefits. That is what the editors of *Webster's New World Dictionary* should have done; but they chose rather, to give this word legitimacy by timidly concealing idolatrous belief.

Webster's definition of **fortune** conceals the idolatrous belief of Roman antiquity, but it accurately reflects current belief. Still today, there are many that seek to make a legitimate claim about a god-like power we now call **fortune.** The utilization of **fortune**, as it is defined currently, continues to elevate and legitimize the identical power that was traditionally associated with the goddess Fortuna. In history, Fortuna claimed to bestow prosperity; today, **fortune** is said to bestow it.

⌘⌘⌘⌘

Another aspect of Fortuna worship that has remained a substantial element in our word **fortune** has to do with future expectations. *Webster's New World Dictionary's* second usage of **fortune** is:

2. What happens or is going to happen to one; one's lot, good or bad; especially one's future lot. [7]

Those who worshipped Fortuna came to her with their hopes and expectations and laid them before her feet, so to speak. They were expecting this goddess to grant their request at some point in the future. They were looking desperately to a future fulfillment of their desires and requests. This "future expectation" concept has survived and remains a current part of *Webster's* modern definition for **fortune.**

No Such Thing As Luck

What developed around Fortuna worship became a belief system that was built upon her alluring promises. After fulfilling their required sacrificial duties, Fortuna's disciples became hopeful. They believed the power of this goddess would bring their requests to pass at a future time. They looked expectantly to her ability. Fortuna's credibility, however, only lived in the confused and twisted minds of those who bowed to her worthless image. Those who worshipped this worthless goddess were participating in an empty, meaningless insanity that led to their personal despair. Fortuna promised, but she never produced, leaving behind disappointed, despondent disciples.

Clearly, groundless pagan religious believing that hopes in a "future expectation," remains a substantial part of the modern conception of **fortune**. Frequently, people attribute what is going to happen in their future to the blessing of **fortune's** power. They embrace the validity of **fortune's** power and they hope in the future rewards that power will bring. They actually believe the power of **fortune** can be a determining factor in what lies ahead. Statements like the following, express their future expectations:

"With good **fortune** I can win the lottery."

"I hope I am **fortunate** enough to get that promotion."

We often hear people speak of themselves as having received a blessing by the hand of **fortune**. Obviously, when individuals confess, "It has been my good **fortune**." they name themselves the benefactor of **fortune's** power. Conversely, we hear individuals referring to themselves as unfortunate, or the recipient of **misfortune**. When people name themselves in this manner, in effect, they are describing how **fortune's** power has been withheld from them – they have not been favored by **fortune's** blessing.

Our modern conception of **fortune** is altogether as faulty as the faulty goddess Fortuna. Fortuna never delivered a single "future expectation," nor can the presumed force, now called **fortune,** deliver. The fallacy of **fortune** is blatantly clear. It is a fake and powerless force; just like Fortuna. It has absolutely nothing to do with what has happened or is going to happen in the future. Both sordid, idolatrous concepts, the ancient version of Fortuna, and her modern-day equivalent, **fortune,** projects empty, worthless, unfulfilled promises.

⌘⌘⌘⌘

Our "future expectations" must be based upon a solid, sure foundation. There are some that would like us to believe our future is out of our personal control. There are also those who believe life is going to kick them around indiscriminately. There are others who believe they are held captive by circumstances. None of this is true. Personal responsibility is the ultimate garment every person must wear. Saint or sinner, it makes no difference; what we choose to believe about our future, what we choose to confess with our mouths, and what we choose to do with our lives, determines our tomorrows. Individual responsibility has always been absolute.

No Such Thing As Luck

Your personal success or failure is your own doing and not another man's. It is only you that can alter your condition. Your personal choices, which are the results of your personal beliefs, brought you to where you are today. It is what you believe in your heart and confess with your mouth that will determine all your tomorrows. The words of Jesus Christ have established this truth:

> For verily I say unto you, That whosoever shall say unto this mountain, Be thou removed, and be thou cast into the sea; and shall not doubt in his heart, but shall believe that those things which he saith shall come to pass; he shall have whatsoever he saith.
>
> Therefore I say unto you, What things soever ye desire, when ye pray, believe that ye receive *them*, and ye shall have *them*.
>
> Mark 11:23-24

We cannot confess belief in a god-like power called **fortune** and then with our next breath call upon our Heavenly Father to bless us with benefits. We cannot have it both ways. God will not share His glory with the idolatrous concept we call **fortune**. God will not share His praise and honor with any faulty, man-made precept. Never is He pleased with erected idols that live in our minds.

⌘⌘⌘⌘

We need to recognize the idolatrous concept of **fortune** for what it is in reality. The concept of **fortune's** power rests squarely upon the idolatrous foundation of a powerless Roman goddess, and nothing more. It is a little difficult to rename the graphic imagery portrayed in the bestowing of benefits from the hand of a Roman goddess. Despite this difficulty, Fortuna has been given a new name, and that name is **fortune**.

In *Webster's* third and fourth usages of **fortune**, we are going to see another abrupt distortion of emphasis. These two usages are given as follows:

3. good luck; success; prosperity
4. wealth; riches; large estate; extensive possessions: [8]

Notice that "good luck", in usage three, is a repeat of what was given earlier in usage one, so it is not a valid, different sense of **fortune**. By excluding the use of "good luck," usages three and four are then essentially the same. Both usages three and four deal with the same subject, and are in fact, the same sense.

In this new sense of **fortune**, *Webster's New World Dictionary* changed the emphasis from the presumed force bestowing the benefits to the benefits themselves. Wealth, riches, prosperity, success, large estate, and extensive possessions are qualities now said to actually be **fortune** itself. The rule of thumb for any good definition of words requires the defining words to equal the word defined. Does *Webster's Dictionary* mean these defining qualities, named here, are **fortune** itself? Yes, that is exactly what is stated! These qualities, these attributes, are now called **fortune** itself, as shown in the only example given:

as, she inherited a fortune. [9]

This newer definition of **fortune** has come to equal wealth and riches, and thusly, wealth and riches equal **fortune**. What a drastic change!

Of course, this new usage of **fortune** is an outright distortion of the original word's meaning. What we saw earlier in the worship of Fortuna was the qualities and attributes bestowed were not themselves Fortuna. But, the benefits supposedly came as a result of Fortuna's decision to bestow them. The benefits did not cause the goddess, rather the goddess was thought to be the cause of the benefits. The newer distorted sense of **fortune** takes the emphasis away from the pagan goddess.

The newer sense of **fortune** is faulty, and without justification. Good success, riches, and wealth always come as a result of something. They do not just float around in space. They have no mind or life of their own, nor do they just happen. The pagan Romans believed these benefits came from a goddess. We know they did not. God is the ultimate source and the true bestower of benefits and blessings. The ancient Romans mistakenly identified Fortuna as the source of their blessings; however, they never depicted their blessings to just aimlessly float around in space.

This striking change in the meaning of **fortune** has made it a casual term. Generally, people are at home with its use. It is clear, however, this word's new meaning is a "cover-up."

Fortune's new meaning only conceals Fortuna's identity as the supplier and the source for benefits. Although the new sense for **fortune** is called wealth—success—and riches, the mystical power of an assumed force still looms close by. You can call a stinkbug by any name you choose, but the stinkbug of idolatry will always stink!

⌘⌘⌘⌘

The introduction of adjectives and other noun forms of **fortune** have developed. These forms appear in most of our dictionaries today. Words such as **fortunate, fortuity** and **fortuitous** are all derived from the exact same Latin root word *fortana*. These newer word forms have nothing new to add; everything that has been said concerning the concept of **fortune** applies to them. They are not new words in relationship to our study. They are only new forms of the same root concept we have already covered. The imagery of Fortuna remains the fundamental basis for the meaning of **fortunate, fortuity**, and **fortuitous.**

It is interesting that some people who choose to use the word **fortunate** would not use the word **lucky**. This is true because the pagan meaning of **fortunate** has been disguised by the corruption of its etymology. Actually, the use of **fortunate** is only a different word that stands for the meaning of **luck**. (It might not hurt any of us to think more seriously about the words we choose to use.)

To be sure, the English language is constantly changing. There are modern anachronistic developments that seek to add legitimacy to the words we are confronting. The introduction of the word "accidental" in defining **fortuitous** is an example of this tendency. Take a look at *Webster's New World Dictionary*; it uses the added concept of accident in defining **fortuitous**.

> Fortuitous: happening by chance; accidental,
> —SYN. see accidental. [10]

Originally, the concept of accident had little to do with this word. Accident, as it is used today, is an added concept that has an unjustified meaning for a definition of **fortuitous**. In Roman mythology, Fortuna did not accidentally give a benefit. She (supposedly) chose to give a benefit. Accident generally refers to a happening that is not intended.

⌘⌘⌘⌘

Webster's New World Dictionary finishes its definition for **fortune** with a reference to fortune telling. The explanation of to "tell one's **fortune**" is as follows:

> To profess to tell what is going to happen in one's life, as by palmistry, cards, etc. [11]

It is not surprising, the concept of **fortune** lends support to the enterprise of fortune telling. Actually, this is the very concept upon which fortune telling is built.

When people are drawn into accepting and embracing the concept of **fate, destiny, lot,** and **fortune**, the next thing they are in line for is the spiritualism of divination called fortune telling. Remember that the basic yearning of those who worshipped Fortuna was to know what lay ahead in the future. Within their mind-set, this goddess was going to determine specific future outcomes. The priests representing and serving this goddess were believed to be the best qualified to predict what a future outcome might be.

Fortuna's priests professed to be versed in their knowledge and ability to predict what the future held. As we studied in the previous chapter, there have been select groups of people throughout history who claim to be versed with this ability to tell the future. They are called by various names: prophets, priests, diviners, et cetera. The *Encyclopedia Americana*, under the listing of fortune telling, lists twenty-three different types or varieties of these people. Here are just a few names by which they are called: chartomancy (divination by cards); cleromancy (divination by lots); crystallomancy (divination by crystals); oneiromancy (divination by dreams); scyphomancy (divination by reading tea leaves). [12] They may be called by different names, but they all, without exception, lay a claim to the same distorted truth. They all claim the ability to tell the future or to predict a given outcome of events. They profess a supernatural gift that will enable them to see what is ahead; to know the future. But, all this is just an illusion; it is a fake. The information they project about the future is fake and the glorying they project of themselves is worthless vanity.

All fortune telling is deception and craftiness. Those who seek to know the future by the mouth of a median are deceived. The median's boastful showmanship and alluring promises are entrapments. Those who seek after a median never gain what they seek. Not only do they fail to gain, but also they suffer loss. Their pockets are emptied by the profit-seeking median. There is almost always a price or a fee required in exchange for the median's fake revelation. Fortune telling has always been a moneymaking racket, and it continues in that same mode today.

The truth is that money is not the greatest loss that people suffer when they are enticed by a fortune-teller. Often they are seduced and fooled by lying signs and wonders. They become persuaded by entrapments. They accept and bow to devilish reasoning and doctrines. They begin to believe the lying predictions and lying explanations they are offered. By remaining ignorant of Satan's devices, their lives are opened to devilish destruction.

The median is also deceived. The activity, centering on fortune telling, is frequently under the control of devil spirits. The devil spirits run the show, so to speak. The median, in effect, relinquishes his or her mental facilities to a controlling, devil spirit. That spirit then proceeds to speak forth lying predictions and deceitful revelations by the mouth of the median. The goal and design of these lying spirits is to work the works and purposes of the devil — namely to kill, steal and destroy.

Devil spirits are boastful deceivers. They make big predictions of the future, but they are limited in their knowledge. They know nothing more of future events than that which God's Word reveals. They can not predict the future anymore than you can. So, the entire operation of fortune telling is a set-up.

Fortune telling has always been a counterfeit of true prophecy and revelation. Idolatrous gods never speak, nor do they provide revelation and information. Pagan priests and prophets falsely claimed to have received revelation and information from the gods that they served, but they never did. Any supposed information received by them was, in reality, from their own making, or of a devilish origin. Satanic revelation has always been deceitful information. Devilish revelation, in the form of lying signs and wonders, is entrapment. Its purpose is both deceptive and destructive.

⌘ ⌘ ⌘ ⌘

The ultimate question concerning the concept of **fortune** is a simple one. Does a legitimate force called **fortune** exist, and does it bestow benefits upon individuals? The answer is emphatically, "NO!" Such a force does not exist today, nor did it ever exist in history. It is obvious, there were men in history that proclaimed the existence of such a power, and there are those today who continue the same claim. They proclaim **fortune** to be an active, living force. Their words, however, are only the misleading, empty claims of men who rejoice in the words of men. They offer empty, lying words to back up their useless claims. The promoters of this false concept have slyly sought to usurp the praise, love, and reverence due to God, our Heavenly Father.

The underlying, deceitful motive that promotes the concept of **fortune** is, in fact, outright rebellion against God. Beliefs and proclamations about the entity of **fortune** are geared to undermine God's Word and to rob God of the honor and praise He is due. They vainly attribute what is in reality God's power and ability, to the presumed entity called **fortune**.

The claim and promise of Fortuna was always that <u>she</u> had the power to bestow a blessing. The big claim and promise in the modern concept of **fortune** is <u>it</u> has the power to bestow a blessing. The change, which deserves our attention, is that Fortuna today is no longer called a <u>she</u>. In her modern form, Fortuna has been transformed into an it – **fortune**. This gender change accommodates Fortuna's disguise and modern day secrecy. People can now feel comfortable referring to our word **fortune** as "it." But nothing has really changed within the heart and guts of this concept's meaning.

Behind our modern designation, which calls **fortune** an "it," remains the ridiculous idolatry of the goddess Fortuna. Her disguised identity continues to call out to men and women, boys and girls: "I have the power to bestow a blessing; believe in my power; call upon my ability; I will protect you; I will bless you with the outcome you so desire in your life." Whatever she is called, a "she" or an "it," the concept behind Fortuna remains an outrageous lie. Claims about ultimate powers are serious. They need to be addressed and answered honestly. The true and everlasting source of power and blessing in the universe is that which belongs to and proceeds forth from our loving God. The critical, life and death question just never changes. Whose word are we going to believe? Will we believe God's Word, or will we believe the preposterous word of those who falsely name **fortune** to be the great source of power and blessing?

Unlike the false, powerless gods of men, our Heavenly Father has ultimate power; He has ability; He is able and sufficient. He has always been and remains the only true source of blessings.

> Every good gift and every perfect gift is from
> above, and cometh down from the Father of
> lights, with Whom is no variableness, neither
> shadow of turning.
>
> James 1:17

Every good gift and every perfect gift, God gives. He is the source behind the gift. He is the force that brings the gift to pass. It is by His hand and by His discretion that a blessing is given.

Starting with Adam and Eve, God blessed them.

> And God blessed them, and God said unto
> them, Be fruitful, and multiply, and replenish
> the earth, and subdue it: and have dominion
> over the fish of the sea, and over every living
> thing that moveth upon the earth.
>
> Genesis 1:28

Upon Abraham's life God invoked a blessing.

> And I will make thee a great nation, and I will
> bless thee, and make thy name great; and thou
> shalt be a blessing:
>
> And I will bless them that bless thee, and curse
> him that curseth thee: and in thee shall all
> families of the earth be blessed.
>
> Genesis 12:2-3

Abraham was the recipient of God's blessing. God prospered his way.

175

No Such Thing As Luck

Throughout human history, God has always been the bestower of blessings:

> For He [God] maketh His sun to rise on the evil and on the good, and sendeth rain on the just and on the unjust.
>
> Matthew 5:45b

God's purpose and design is to be a bestower of "blessedness." His outstretched hand of blessings reaches into every category of human life.

> Blessed *be* the God and Father of our Lord Jesus Christ, Who hath blessed us with all spiritual blessings in heavenly *places* in Christ:
>
> Ephesians 1:3

God's "blessedness" upon our lives is awesome. It is just too big to fully grasp:

> He is our plenty and our protection.
> He is our refuge and our safety.
> He is gracious and forgiving.
> He is our strength and our helper.
> He exalts us and sits us on high places.
> He is our supplier and our sure reward.
> He is our rejoicing and our glory.
> He is our wisdom.
> He is our redeemer.
> He heals us and makes us whole.
> It is by Him that we triumph in this life and in all eternity.

God bestows every good and every perfect gift. He confers it by His will. He invokes it; it is by His hand and by His discretion that it comes to pass for us personally. There is no other sure source of blessings.

Why would anyone ever look to the falsehood of the disguised god we now call **fortune**? Why would anyone ever bow to this meaningless concept and look hopelessly to it for the blessings of life? All we need do is look to our wonderful God; He stands ready to fulfill our every human need. He is truly the Rock of All Ages.

> O come, let us sing unto the Lord: let us make a joyful noise to the rock of our salvation.
>
> Let us come before His presence with thanksgiving, and make a joyful noise unto Him with psalms.
>
> For the Lord *is* a great God, and a great King above all gods.
> Psalms 95:1-3

No Such Thing As Luck

[1]   Securdus, Gaius Plinius, *Natural History*, Loeb Classical Library, Cambridge, Mass., 1957, p. II22

[2]   *Political Calculus: Essay on Machiavelli's Philosophy*, [Concept of Fortuna in Machiavelli by Thomas Flanagan] UMI Books on Demand, MI, 1997, ed. Anthony Parel, p. 130

[3]   *New Larousse Encyclopedia of Mythology*, Introduction by Robert Graves, Hamlyn Publishing Co., NY, 1977, p. 213

[4]   The *Barnhart Dictionary of Etymology*, ed. Robert K. Barnhart, 1988, s.v. "Fortuna" reprinted with permission from The H.W. Wilson Company

[5]   *Webster's New World Dictionary*, The World Publishing Co., NY, 1968, s.v. "fortune"

[6]   Ibid, s.v. "Fortuna"

[7]   Ibid., s.v. "fortune"

[8]   Ibid.

[9]   Ibid.

[10]   Ibid, s.v. "fortuitous"

[11]   Ibid, s.v. "fortune"

[12]   *Encyclopedia Americana*, 1962 Edition, s.v. "Fortunetelling"

"If we are going to understand the true meaning of **chance**, we must understand the vocabulary that surrounds it."

CHAPTER NINE

Chances Are?
There are No Chances Are!

If we were searching for a theme song for this chapter, the 1950's hit tune, "Chances Are", might make a good one. Lyrics from this well-known song express some of the popular thinking associated with the notion of **chance**. The song projects the idea that the force of **chance** is working actively in a romantic attraction between a fellow and his girl. However, the category of romance is only one of many that is thought to be influenced by the power of **chance**. The concept of **chance** is fully accepted and used without reserve. People believe **chance** is a reality, that it exists. Just who questions the idea of it? Its meaning is common knowledge. It generally means the absence of cause; a happening or **luck**. Most of us are also very familiar with the over-all context in which the concept is used. Here are a few phrases with which almost everyone will be familiar: a good **chance**; fat **chance**; **chances** are; take my **chances**; second **chance**; by **chance**; and what are the **chances**? What we need to do in this chapter is search out both the depth of its meaning and use.

Chance provides the whimsical, fickle nature in its relationship with **fate** — **chance** may, or it may not, who can tell? Its concept, however, has outgrown the confinement of **fate's** meaning. As we will soon see, **chance** stands upon its own feet and projects some new and enlarged meanings today. We are going to leave nothing to **chance** in this chapter! As a matter of fact, the prospect of dethroning this popular concept is excellent.

The action in the words **fate, destiny,** and **lot**, is that of an outside force acting upon the individual. The concept of **chance** changes the point of action away from the outside influence of a god working upon an individual. In the concept of **chance,** the action is with the individual himself, who is doing both the observing and the explaining. The action of this word questions what is going to occur. Watch for this point of emphasis change in the following definitions of **chance** from *Webster's New World Dictionary*:

> **chance** (chans, chäns), *n.* [ME. *chance, chaunce*; OFr. *cheance*; LL. *cadentia,* that which falls out; L. *cadens,* ppr. of *cadere,* to fall], 1. the way things happen or turn out. 2. apparent absence of cause or design; fortuity; luck; often personified. 3. a happening; fortuitous event; accidental circumstance. 4. a risk or gamble. 5. a share in a lottery. 6. an opportunity: as, you'll have a *chance* to go. 7. a possibility or

probability: as, there is a *chance* that he will
live. –SNY. see happen, random. [1]

Chance (*cadere*) is traceable in its Latin form to before
1300 A.D., and its concept goes in a straight line back to
Roman idolatry. In the idolatrous world of the Romans, the
casting forth and the "falling out" of the **lot** was considered
a spiritual activity. The **lot,** as we know, was used in an effort
to obtain a message from a god. That which fell out did so,
supposedly, by the direction of a deity. We saw in an earlier
chapter, the casting forth of **lots** was serious business for the
Romans. The essential aspect for them was the message
obtained by the casting down of the **lot,** and not the **lot**
itself. With this in mind, it is easy to see the "falling out"
sense of *cadere* refers to the message being sought. Exactly
what was the message from the god going to be; how was
the decision of a god going to "fall out?" That is what they
wanted to know.

The truer sense of *cadere* must be seen as a question about
a future development — that which is going to happen. Its
action rests altogether upon the question, "What?" *Cadere,*
in its original sense, was dealing with a future occurrence
and asking "what" is going to come to pass? What is going
to "fall out" concerning some event? For example: "Will my
grain crop prosper this year? It is up to the gods! So, which
way will this event turn out? What will the gods do? Out of
the possibilities, which one is going to 'fall out'? What is
going to happen?" Questions about the "will of the gods"
produced the concept of "*cadere*" or **chance.** The Latin term,
cadere or *cadentia* in its predicate form, referred to the
possibilities of what was going to "fall out" upon a human

life. The emphasis of this word was simply dealing with possibilities; the possibilities of what would occur.

⌘⌘⌘⌘

The Latin word *cadentia* forwarded the aspect of establishing theological possibilities – what might the gods do? The French word for **chance**, *cleance*, forwarded only a part of the meaning from the Latin *cadentia*. They dropped the religious aspect of the Latin word. The French concept of **chance** dealt with the possible outcome of events, but with little or no reference to the cause behind the events. In the French word, "unknown causes" replaced deities. This was a big change. It was also a tremendous departure from the Latin, *cadentia*'s, theological meaning.

The French were not involved with ancient Roman idolatry. It is easy to see why they left off the Roman theological context. The French were, however, involved in secular humanism. The pervasive, secular humanism of the French, during the Middle Ages, tended to exclude the working of God's power. Ideas and beliefs about theological causes did not interest them. They began to foster concepts of unknown causes.

The absence of a theological significance in the French word *cleance* opened a trap door. This is how the unsound thinking of agnosticism walked straight into their meaning of **chance**. The agnostics propounded that it is impossible to know anything other than material phenomena. This very logic became the foundational reasoning that developed the

French meaning of **chance**. The French understanding for this word centers upon possibilities, but without regard to causes. The same agnostic reasoning, which is engrained in the French concept of **chance**, remains active in our use and understanding of this word today.

Secular humanism continues to leave God out of the cause and effect realities of life. Humanistic veins of thought have prompted teachings declaring that God has removed His presence and power from certain spheres of life altogether. Certain circumstances and categories of life are said to remain outside of God's control and influence. The supposed absence of God's influence in these spheres of life has left decision-making to some unknown, obscure force. This mysterious vacuum of activity, from which God has supposedly excluded Himself, is a category of life where anything could or might happen – it is really "iffy." Since no one knows what this "godless force" will do, or refrain from doing, the outcome in this sphere of activity is questionable.

It is the outcome of events emanating from this supposed "godless sphere" that many declare to be matters of **chance**. This is the concept of **chance** that has been developed by the unsound logic of agnostic humanism. In its second and third definitions of **chance**, *Webster's New World Dictionary* reflects this humanistic logic and belief:

> (2) apparent absence of cause or design; fortuity; luck: often personified and (3) a happening; fortuitous event; accidental circumstance.[2]

Sadly, approval and acceptance of this wayward logic is wholeheartedly embraced by our society today. They have bought into its use and they continue to embrace its worthless meaning.

⌘⌘⌘⌘

The French also developed the idea of "likelihood" in association with **chance** theories. Their definition of **chance** came to include the idea of likelihood in relationship to the possible outcome of events, or the likelihood of **chance** possibilities. Several of their leading mathematicians undertook the activity of analyzing various games of **chance**. Probability Theories developed by Blaise Pascal and Pierre de Fermat in the mid seventeenth century were used to determine the possible outcomes of dice cast in games of **chance.**

> The problem Pascal was trying to solve concerned the division of the stakes and the value of each throw; i.e. Points assigned to each throw of the dice." [3]

> Such games as the tossing of dice or coins and the drawing of balls from urns continued for a long time to serve as the chief models for the construction of probability theory. [4]

The activities of these men centered on ascribing a numerical value (the likelihood) to the outcome (the various possibilities) in a toss of the dice.

Chances Are?

Probability theory, as developed by Pascal and Fermat, has been redefined through the centuries. Today, scientists consider statistical and mathematical probability methods, essential tools. The credibility of probability science is generally assumed. Its broad acceptance has led to extensive use. Its use is no longer confined to science. Probability theory is also used in business, politics, and the social spectrum. Decision-making in American government is determined, in large measure, by probability methods and formulas.

The probability vocabulary developed by mathematicians, scientists, and philosophers over the centuries has become familiar to us. We have grown accustomed to using probability terminology without thinking much about the specialized language it projects. The following is a partial list of the specialized probability vocabulary we have grown accustomed to hearing:

Likely	Circumstances	Event
Equally likely	Cause	Odds
Frequency	Relevance	Classes
Random	Reasonable	Finite set
Risk	Relative frequency	Inference
Occurrence	Favorable case	Sampling
Supposed	Numerical value	

Most of these terms are used in public opinion poll formulas. Random sampling polls reach into almost any category of life. Politicians rely upon polls. Political polling goes on constantly. Random sampling methods are used extensively in business sales to establish potential markets. Advertisers use polls to target their audience.

No Such Thing As Luck

⌘⌘⌘⌘

No category of life and living is off limits to modern day opinion polls. Pollsters might devise questions about anything from soup to sex. A good example of how far out of bounds survey polling has gotten can be seen in the news media's use of them, which is quick to air the results of its personal surveys. It has successfully latched onto the "image of accuracy" projected by the scientific community's use of probability theory.

We often hear those in the media talk about "dedication to the public interest." What we frequently observe, however, is its hypocrisy in utilizing sampling polls to "make the news." Its polling activity is employed as a powerful tool to persuade public opinion and to justify its political causes. Their polling activity may appear to be very legitimate; but accuracy is not their goal. Accuracy is only the image the news media hopes to project. Actually, deceitful manipulation of the polling process is not uncommon among news journalists. Many of their polling practices are designed to produce a result they desire. Survey questions are craftily worded to produce just the right response they hope to gain. Their lying surveys undermine their self-proclaimed "truthful image." And who is fooled by their hypocrisy?

Darrell Huff, in his book, *How to Lie with Statistics*, exposed some of the misuse in this field. In a review, which appeared on Amazon.com, Darrell Huff's book on statistics is characterized as follows:

Amazon.com:

"There is terror in numbers," writes Darrell Huff in *How to Lie with Statistics*. And nowhere does this terror translate to blind acceptance of authority more than in the slippery world of averages, correlations, graphs, and trends. Huff sought to break through "the daze that follows the collision of statistics with the human mind" with this slim volume, first published in 1954. The book remains relevant as a wake-up call for people unaccustomed to examining the endless flow of numbers pouring from Wall Street, Madison Avenue, and everywhere else someone has an axe to grind, a point to prove, or a product to sell. "The secret language of statistics, so appealing in a fact-minded culture, is employed to sensationalize, inflate, confuse, and oversimplify," warns Huff.

From *Book News, Inc.*:

A 1954 classic that continues to dispel false beliefs and inform the statistically naïve. Huff's direct and witty style exposes how advertisers, government, and the media misled their audiences through the misuse of statistics. Huff then explains how the reader can see through the smoke and mirrors to get to the real meaning – if any- of what is presented. [5]

No Such Thing As Luck

Obviously, the impending need is to discredit the phony documentation presented by news journalists, and anyone else, choosing to employ the shady practice of survey deceit.

⌘⌘⌘⌘

Space will not allow us to treat the entire specialized vocabulary used in **chance** theory. We do, however, need to take a short look at some of these important words. If we are going to understand the true meaning of **chance**, we must understand the vocabulary that surrounds it. Risk is one of those words, and we hear it used often.

RISK comes to us from the French word *risqué* and its basic meaning refers to the **chance** of injury, damage, or loss (danger). [6] The term is utilized extensively in both the fields of business and insurance. Within this context, the concept of risk seeks to assign a numerical value to a possible unwanted outcome. It seeks to numerically establish the amount of risk at stake. The overall concept of risk, though, is much broader than its usage by the insurance industry. In order to understand the meaning of risk we need to understand the cause behind the risk, or the cause for the risk. A word used to define risk can help us; it is danger.

The word <u>danger</u> originally referred to the absolute power of an overlord. Power, domination, and arrogance are associated with its meaning. Danger has finally come to mean the ability or power to cause injury, damage, loss, pain, or peril. [7] In a shortened sense, danger means —the ability to work evil upon. This meaning of danger fits well with the meaning of risk. Risk refers to vulnerability, and the meaning of danger names the reason for that vulnerability – a dominating evil power. As we can now see, the fuller meaning of risk is vulnerability to a dominating evil force.

The meaning of risk acknowledges the existence of an evil force, powerful enough to work harm upon us. It also admits to being vulnerable to that power, and it seeks to understand what this powerful, negative force is going to do. It is plain to see that the concept of risk has not gotten away from the ancient idolatrous question the Romans asked about their gods, "What are they going to do?" Idolatrous Romans believed in the existence of powerful gods who could work evil upon them. They confessed their vulnerability to these supposed powers, and they sought to know exactly what their gods were going to do. A good question to ask might be, "How does the concept of risk differ from the idolatrous belief system of the Romans?" The only major difference is that the Romans bowed down upon their knees to worship their idols. Idolaters today, bow in their hearts. They embrace the negativity embodied in the idea of risk. They confess subjugation to an evil power, and they want to know what this power is going to do. When we look at the cause behind the meaning of risk, it is easy to see this word's idolatrous nature.

The word "risk" admits to the existence of a dark power, and it calls the questionable behavior of this power, **chance**. The meaning of risk also seeks to name the possibilities of what may or may not come to pass. It longs to know what will come to pass, but it cannot know. Probability theory predicts "<u>what</u> will come to pass," but the concept of risk is limited to only projections about what "<u>may</u> come to pass." Risk attempts to name the possibilities. This is where talk of "the odds" comes into play.

No Such Thing As Luck

⌘⌘⌘⌘

ODDS, is another specialized vocabulary word associated with probability and **chance**. We have all heard this question, "What are the odds?" Well, here we go again! Try as we may, we have still not gotten away from the "what" question. In its usage with the odds, the question "what" is seeking to establish a numerical value. It is asking, "What are the **chances** of a specific outcome?" "What are the odds?" is really the question; "What is the degree of favorability for one event as opposed to the other?" Odds making, is no different from the probability method used in science. In fact, the setting of odds is the utilization of a probability method.

We are all very familiar with the use of "the odds" in betting and gambling. Gambling (taking a **chance**) is a vast industry affecting our culture. Corrupted state legislators have made the operation of a lottery legal in numerous states across the nation. Sports' betting continues to flourish. Gambling centers like Las Vegas, Atlantic City, Biloxi, Mississippi, and others around the nation, continue to rake in their enormous profits from so called "games of **chance**." Showgirls, bright lights, enticing amenities, and the ever-present crafty delusions of "getting something for nothing," lure millions to these Big Name Gambling Centers. How many of these operations do you know that have gone out of business?

The closed-set probability formulas utilized by the gaming industry enable them to secure enormous profits. By the utilization of "large number scenario formulas," they successfully calculate the great advantage they enjoy. They insure that the vast numbers of the individuals playing their so-called "games of **chance**" will lose. They need losers to make their profits, and they are the experts at making losers. Odds are said to equalize the **chances** favoring one as opposed to the other. The system is out of balance. The advantage enjoyed by the gaming industry far outweighs that of the participants. **Chance** has nothing to do with anything in the gaming industry. Strictly speaking, the setting of odds is nothing more than the difference between the assignment of numerical values. At its best, the practice remains questionable. Maybe it is time for serious minded men and women to reexamine the soundness of probability theory's widespread use. Exactly when can probability's science be sensibly applied?

⌘⌘⌘⌘

Limited, or closed-set probability theories, operating under strictly controlled environments, can make projections with some degree of certainty. Outside of a "closed-set" environment, however, the assignment of numerical values is subjective. In the general realm of life, there are very few "closed sets." This is especially true in the social categories. The possibilities are uncontrollable here – even uncountable. Futile efforts to define the ratio of outcomes to the possibilities, in this category, ought to be seriously questioned. You may call it whatever you choose – odds or probability — but the information at hand is the critical requirement.

Sound conclusions about the possible outcome of events are contingent upon truthful information. Nothing is going to be accurate without truthfulness. The breakdown by the pollsters in the 2000 presidential election is a good example of polling failure. The national polling firm employed by the news networks failed to produce accurate projections. They failed to gather truthful information and they erred in their projected winner for the state of Florida.

Another example of a futile survey study is one conducted by the National Crime Victims Research and Treatment Center at the Medical University of South Carolina in 1992. According to this study:

> Nationally, 84 percent of sexual assault victims do not go to police, most out of fear people will learn about the assault or that they will be blamed for the attack. [8]

How arrogant can researchers become? No closed-set probability formula could produce accuracy in such a study. How vain and misleading surveys and polling have become.

The specialized language of probability theory confounds the general public. Odds setting and probability projections have grabbed up people's docile acceptance and have taken them on a deceptive journey. People tend to bank on this suspect information and mistakenly rely upon it in critical decision making. They remain enamoured by its scientifically projected image of authority and credibility. In the end, it is far more important to look to the motivation and truthfulness of those who are employing the probability method than to be carried away by its present day aura of broad acceptance.

⌘⌘⌘⌘

In addition to examining the probability vocabulary, we also need to look at another aspect of probability theory. We need to see how **chance** and probability science are interrelated. The continuity and uniformity of the universe's design does make it possible to use known information about a property to project possible outcomes for unknown properties. This is a legitimate use of probability theory. It is essential, however, to understand and to remember probability theory deals with the operation of **chance**. Probability theory is **chance** theory.

It may seem a little strange in our "scientific-minded society" to talk about **chance** theory, but probability science allows the validity of **chance**. To much of the scientific community, probability absolutely implies **chance**, and so it should. By looking carefully at the "equally likely" term used in probability theory, anyone can see its reference is to the concept of **chance**. "Likely" suggests probability. Probability in this context implies **chance**. "Equally likely," as used in probability theory, basically means "of the same **chance**," and can have no other rightful meaning. Equally implies in an equal manner, i.e., equal (of the same **chance**).

195

No Such Thing As Luck

> The science of statistics is permeated with the ideas of the theory of chance, from the first steps in collecting the data to the drafting of the final conclusions of investigation.... The finished product of statistics is usually a table of chances. [9]

According to the above quote, the true spirit of statistics is governed by **chance** theory.

Kenneth R. Atkins textbook, entitled *Physics*, has a chapter dealing with probability and uncertainty. His discussion concerning the directional factors influencing an electron has this to say:

> The future behavior of an electron is not completely determined by its past history. Several possibilities are available for its future behavior and one of these is chosen purely by chance, for no reason that can ever be determined. This applies to all aspects of the behavior of an electron. [10]

It is interesting that nowhere outside of probability theory does the scientific community ever leave anything to **chance**. Investigation of cause and effect is, in fact, the renowned standard of modern science. Cause and effect form the postulate of the scientific method; but probability language has masked the concept of **chance** and given it a respectable face. So, the doctrine of **chance** continues to live. It is alive and doing well within the respectable mask of probability science.

Chances Are?

The method of probability science is complex because it has established a complicated vocabulary that lacks clarity and simplicity. Its mathematical and philosophical postulates and definitions are confusing and beyond common understanding. The conclusions drawn by probability science are easy to spot because the conclusions produced by this method utilizes key words that have been given extended meanings beyond their standard dictionary definitions.

Look for these pivotal words in the newspapers and television reports of polls and surveys. Here are a few of these specialized words to keep in mind:

incidents of	more likely	favorable
unlikely	random sample	odds
equally likely	greater frequency of	likelihood
occurrence of	greater opportunity of	likely

The conclusion of probability theory would be difficult to express without these "loaded" words and their extended meanings. The value of what probability theory concludes, outside of the natural sciences, should be examined carefully and with due caution. This is especially needful in the social categories.

⌘⌘⌘⌘

Philosophical arguments claiming validity for the concept of **chance** are as old as the philosophers themselves. Aristotle,

No Such Thing As Luck

John Stuart Mill, and Ardigo all regarded **chance** events to be those occurring at the intersection of independent causal chains. For example: an unexpected meeting of a friend in the marketplace was a **chance** event. In the case of Epicurus, Lucretius, Cournot, and Peirce, **chance** meant an uncaused happening. For example: the swerving of an atom by its own inner power would be a matter of **chance**. [11]

Arguments and philosophical justifications, vindicating **chance** theory, continue in our day. Most of these modern arguments center on the posturing of terms and the construction of definitions. Many of these definitions are predicated upon probability theory. What these modern philosophers are justifying is a theoretical measurement of a **chance** occurrence. Their **chance** theory vocabulary includes words and phrases such as the following:

causation	relative frequency
circumstances	statistical inferences
regularities	chance distribution
contingent	quantitative data
reasonable credence	sequence of observations
favorable case	objective probability
objective chance	principles of randomness
potential tendency	dynamical chances

The sophisticated language of this list is designed to justify a philosophical stance. The persuasion of this philosophical stance is that **chance** is real, and the utilization of this vocabulary seeks to cast the supposed reality of **chance** in a favorable light, making its meaning credible.

⌘⌘⌘⌘

We have surveyed a little of the probability and philosophical vocabulary that surrounds the concept of **chance**. There are, however, other commonly used words that either mean or refer to the idea of it. These words have a tremendous baring upon our ability to understand what **chance** truly means. Again, if we are going to establish the real meaning of **chance** we need to take the time, and maintain the patience required to understand the vocabulary used to define it.

We are going to study five of these important words, and we will quickly learn they can easily be called into question; they are unjustifiably used to bolster and bring credibility to the meaning of **chance**. Understanding these words will help us to slide a hangman's noose over the idea of **chance** and choke it to death.

The meaning of **chance** is identified with both opportunity and possibility. *Webster's New World Dictionary* uses both of these words in its definition of **chance**:

6. an opportunity; as, you'll have a *chance* to go
7. a possibility or probability: as, there is a *chance* that he will live. [12]

It is almost unbelievable how many words, in current use, were established within idolatrous practices and beliefs. These words, and the concepts they stand for, have remained a part of our thinking and believing throughout the ages. Perhaps not many of us are aware of the idolatrous foundation upon which these commonly used words were built. The word opportunity owes its origin to the practice of idolatry.

OPPORTUNITY, today, is used most often in the sense of timely or favorable circumstances. (That which is fitting in regard to a purpose). [13] This word, however, developed from the worship of a Roman god named Portunus. He was their god of harbors. [14] Romans attributed the safe and timely arrival of a ship and its cargo to the power of Portunus. If a cargo had arrived safely at harbor, they believed it was the work of this god; it was his doing. They would say it was opportune (blessed by Portunus). It was their acknowledgement of Portunus' supposed power that established the fundamental meaning of our word opportunity. Gradually, the point of emphasis for opportunity changed to the meaning of "favorable circumstances."

The use of opportunity as a defining quality of **chance**, however, opens up the ancient theological aspect of opportune – the blessing of a god! This idolatrous meaning of opportunity has been successfully brought into the definition of **chance**. The meaning of opportunity clarifies the force that is supposedly at work in the concept of **chance**. The operation of **chance** is thereby named to be the action or force of a god - in this case, the god Portunus. This is not new to us, because we have seen this identical, pagan, theological logic rear its ugly head before.

We also need to understand why the word POSSIBILITY has mistakenly been used to define the concept of **chance**.

Chance could only become a possibility if it had the ability to act. For example: "The **chances** are good that it will rain tomorrow", implies that **chance** has the ability to make it rain. It does not! The concept of **chance** only claims power. It claims the "power of determination," but it cannot supply. The most basic meaning we have of **chance** is the understanding of a suspicious "falling out" – that which has been determined by the supposed power of a god. With this in mind, we can begin to see why the word possibility has been mistakenly drawn into the definition of **chance**.

One can truthfully say, "There is a possibility for rain tomorrow," when all the forces, which act to make rain are available. One cannot truthfully say, "There is a **chance** for rain tomorrow," because the power of **chance** cannot make rain or anything else. **Chance** is totally without the power to act. This is why a supportive word, like possibility, has been drawn into its definition. Possibility adds strength to the questionable concept of **chance**. It is used to bolster and fortify the doubtful meaning surrounding it. The word possibility empowers the weak, powerless claim made in the concept of **chance** and attempts to make it credible.

The meaning of possibility deals with the influence that may come to bear upon an event or happening. It is associated with the words: can, able and power. [15] It refers to the capability of an existing power to act. Possibility also implies the fact of existence. When applied to the concept of **chance**, possibility refers to the possible actions of an existing power to bring something to pass. With this meaning of possibility standing by its side, the assumption has now become – **chance** has the power and the ability to act. By using the established meaning of possibility to define **chance**, the meaning of **chance** begins to look like a possibility. The word possibility makes **chance** look credible, but it is not.

No Such Thing As Luck

Chance is not possibility. To claim that **chance** is possibility is more than error, it is a lie. Possibility cannot rightfully define **chance**. To say that **chance** is a possibility is to say that **chance** exists and it has the power to act. None of this meaning is true. Since **chance** is not a possibility, possibility cannot define the meaning of **chance**. **Chance** refers to the questionable action of a supposed "god power." Possibility refers to the existence of a power, as a matter of fact, reality. **Chance** is idolatrous speculation. Possibility is that which God has made available in this life. To say of **chance**, "It is a possibility" refutes the abiding presence of God's power and uplifting love. To call **chance** a possibility only supports the wayward, anemic logic of idolatrous belief.

Space will not allow a full word study for the concepts surrounding the meaning of the words, "ACCIDENT," "CIRCUMSTANCES" and "RANDOM." A brief examination of these three terms is all that is needed to reveal their relationship to **chance**. *Webster's New World Dictionary* uses "accidental circumstance" to define **chance**. Accident is derived from two Latin words: *accidere* – to happen and *cadere* – to fall. [16] We saw earlier that *cadere* refers to the questionable action of Roman gods. Accident was originally associated with the identical idolatry projected in the concept of **chance**. Originally, the concept of accident attempted to name the nature of a god's action. Its meaning sought to show both the cause and the nature of a behavior. Today, this word names unknown causes, careless causes, unintentional causes, and unexpected causes. The over-riding impact of accident's meaning continues to imply that **chance** is an active force working in and among our lives. Accident names the nature of **chance** and seeks to tell us how it behaves.

Circumstance comes from the Latin, *circumstare*, to stand around, from *circum* + stare, to stand. [17] The word makes a presumptive assessment about the reason for a happening or an event. To name the circumstances requires a conclusion about the causes surrounding a matter. Its meaning is both an assumption and a conclusion. The action in circumstance names the associative causes that may surround anything. It both asks and answers the question - "what"; as in, "What are the circumstances?" The question "what" grammatically asks for a specification of an identity. It seeks a truthful explanation to the nature of a thing. To name "what" requires a truthful conclusion.

Whenever the word circumstance is drawn into the definition of **chance,** we are confronting faulty conclusions. To say that "accidental circumstance" is **chance** is more than misleading; it is error. To say that circumstance is **chance,** is to sanction that **chance** exists and that it is a viable force with the ability to influence the activities surrounding our lives. This cannot be true. Whatever the circumstances may be, they will not be fostered nor governed by the supposed force called **chance.** The true forces governing circumstances have absolutely nothing to do with **chance.**

Webster's New World Dictionary gives the word random as a synonym for **chance.** Originally, random meant at great speed – without control. In time, it came to mean a lack of order or disorder. By 1565 A.D., it meant without plan, "at random." [18] This word's association with **chance** is easy to understand. The word random is used to name the sphere of operation for the concept of **chance.** The idea of random describes what **chance** does - how it behaves. Random tells us that **chance** is "iffy," rash, without order or control. However, it is possible to have rash, reckless, out-of-control behavior that is not caused by **chance.** The identical behavior can come from a stubborn mule or a drunken sailor or by many other causes. **Chance** does not cause anything.

No Such Thing As Luck

Today's meaning of random is, "without careful choice."[19] The scientific community, however, has redefined this word to stand for **chance** itself. (Maybe to some scientist, "random" sounds more sophisticated than **chance**.) The following math book's definition of random sample makes it synonymous with, equal **chance**.

> A sample that is representative of the population is often called a random sample. A RANDOM SAMPLE is a sample chosen in such a way that everyone in the population has an equal chance of being in the sample. [20]

It has required a little patience to survey some of the words the dictionary uses to describe the idea of **chance**. Those who care to pursue the study of additional words can review these: contingent, happens, precarious, haphazard, venture, and prospect. The extensive vocabulary, which surrounds the meaning of **chance**, is a witness against its clarity. Numerous dictionaries offer an extensive list of senses for its meaning. No one actually knows what **chance** is, so it has been redefined over and over again through the ages. Its original association with pagan idolatry overshadows any attempt to make it credible. The insanity of its original meaning needs to be brought to light and kept in mind. By doing so, its "new fangled," sophisticated attire will not lead us astray.

---

[1] *Webster's New World Dictionary*, World Pub., Cleveland, OH., 1968, s.v. "chance"

[2] Ibid.

[3] David, F.N., *Games, Gods, and Gambling*, Hafner Pub., NY, 1962, p.83

[4] *Encyclopedia Americana*, Vol. 22, Americana Corp., NY, 1966, s.v. "probability"

[5] Amozon.com - Editorial Review of *How to Lie with Statistics*, viewed 2 Septmember, 2004

[6] *Webster's New World Dictionary*, s.v. "risk"

[7] Ibid., s.v. "danger"

[8] Jon Sarche, "Advocates fear fallout from testimany of Bryant accuser," *Jackson County Floridan*, 24 March 2004, p. 3B

[9] Livinson, Horace C., *Chance, Luck, and Statistics*, Dover Pub., NY, 1963, pp. 218-219

[10] Atkins, Kenneth R., *Physics*, John Wiley and Sons Inc., NY, 1970, p. 563

[11] *Dictionary of Philosophy and Religion*, Ed. W. L. Reese, Humanities Press, New Jersey, 1992, p. 85

[12] *Webster's New World Dictionary*, s.v. "chance"

[13] Ibid. s.v. "opportunity"

[14] *Encyclopedia Americana*, s.v. "Portunus"

[15] *Barnheart Dictionary of Etymology*, Wilson Co., 1988, s.v. "possibility." Reprinted with permission from The H. W. Wilson Company

[16] *Webster's New World Dictionary*, s.v. "accident"

[17] *Merri-Webster Unabridged Dictionary*, s.v. "circumstance"

[18] *Barnhearts*, s.v. "random." Reprinted with permission from The H. W. Wilson Company

[19] *Webster's*, s.v. "random"

[20] *Middle School Math, Course 3*, Scott Foresman-Addison Wesley, CA., 1998, p. 33

"Here is the great truth all of us need to understand. Just no category in life is outside of God's care, God's power, and God's love."

CHAPTER TEN

No Chance for Chance!

Sound thinking has produced a body of information that refutes the concept of **chance**. Throughout history, there have been those who stood in opposition to the whimsical uncertainty of **chance** philosophy. Modern deterministic philosophy accepts that nothing happens by **chance**.

> No matter what happens, there is always a reason why that happened rather than something else. This is called the principle of sufficient reason... determinism asserts that for whatever happens there is always a cause, or that nothing happens by chance....
>
> Now a cause is often defined as both a sufficient and necessary condition for an event

to take place. And determinism may be said to assert that for every event there is both a necessary and a sufficient condition, so that nothing else could have happened other than what did happen.[1]

The renowned Isaac Newton was one of the forerunners of this kind of philosophical thought. Newton's view of the physical universe was that:

The mass, position, and velocity of every particle in the universe constitutes the necessary and sufficient conditions for all natural events. [2]

He believed in cause and effect. In his thinking, determinism was mechanical. Newton's pastor, Samuel Clarke, was himself well versed in this category of thought. These two men had some profitable discussions over the years of their friendship. Dr. Clarke's belief concerning **chance** theory is as follows:

It is strictly and philosophically true in nature and reason that there is no such thing as chance or accident; it being evident that these words do not signify anything really existing, anything that is truly an agent or the cause of any event; but they signify merely men's ignorance of the real and immediate cause. [3]

Dr. Clarke has summed things up in a meaningful way. He looked through all the errors of meaningless philosophy and man-made theology concerning **chance** theory, and concluded **chance** is the cause of nothing. **Chance** theory only signifies man's ignorance concerning the real cause behind an event.

All along in history there have been a few sound-thinking men and women in the scientific community.

> There are those, like the late, Albert Einstein, who felt an inner conviction that reality must ultimately prove somehow to be completely determinate, and who therefore felt that chance, alternative, and probability have no place in its description. [4]

Einstein stood his ground against quantum mechanics theory, which supports the idea of radical, **chance** behavior within the make-up of matter. The modern development of String Theory in Physics is beginning to validate his belief in the coherent unity that exists in the make-up of particles.

> According to string theory, the elementary ingredients of the universe are *not* point particles. Rather, they are tiny, one-dimensional filaments somewhat like infinitely thin rubber bands, vibrating to and fro...Yet the simple replacement of point particles with strands of string as the fundamental ingredients of everything has far-reaching consequences. First and foremost, string theory appears to resolve the conflict between general relativity and quantum mechanics. As we shall see, the spatially extended nature of a string is the crucial new

element allowing for a single harmonious framework incorporating both theories. Second, string theory provides a truly unified theory, since all matter and all forces are proposed to arise from one basic ingredient: oscillating strings. [5]

The theories and philosophies of the best scientific minds have not yet explained the sum and substance for the building blocks of matter. It is a realistic certainty that they never will. That understanding remains God's secret. However, the soundest, most updated information available to us supports cause and effect realities.

⌘⌘⌘⌘

Again, spiritual realities must be considered in order to understand all of the poorly conceived categories that emanate from the idea of **chance**. For example, take the occasion of a man walking into the room of his friend who is sick with infectious hepatitis. What will the outcome be for the man who has come for a visit? There are many that would say **chances** are good that he will get hepatitis. The scientific-minded statistician might say the probability is seventeen cases in 100 for his contacting infectious hepatitis. A gambler might lay odds of six to one for his getting the disease. But, what has really transpired with these three conclusions? All three responses have made a projected guess concerning a future outcome. Their projections might be based on experience, or on averages, or case studies, or even on opinion polls. But they are going to be wrong! These projections, of course, have taken into account every possible factor they knew about. But, they are still going to be wrong! "What was the real outcome for this event?", you ask. This is what happened.

The sick man called his friend to come for a visit. The sick man's friend responded and came. While he was there, he ministered healing in the name of Jesus Christ, and the sick man was immediately healed of his disease. The friend walked out of the hepatitis-infected room in sound health; and the man who was healed of hepatitis walked out of that room with him. In this example, the three responses failed to consider the spiritual realities available to the sick man. Those who made the erroneous conclusions did not understand, or believe, that a miracle of healing was going to take place. Nevertheless, the cause and effect believing of the men in that room accomplished a miracle of deliverance.

Let's take a look at the weather man who daily deals with projections and assumptions. How often do we hear his forecast (a projection of the future) fall by the wayside in error? Actually, his projections are wrong quite often. The well-meaning meteorologist gathers all the available information he can find. He uses the most scientific methods and the most modern upgraded computer system available. His job is to use this information as a basis to predict tomorrow's weather. What has happened when his projection does not come to pass? He has failed to take into account *all* the factors producing the weather for that day. For example, no weather man could have known that Jesus Christ would command the weather to change that day long ago on the Sea of Galilee. When all the correct information is available, a sound conclusion can be projected concerning a future event. But, this is cause and effect. The unknown elements of life are not a matter of so-called **chance**. They remain just a matter of ignorance, and sometimes, plain old unbelief.

It is true that there are many categories of life that give the appearance of **chance**, or the seeming appearance of a **chance** happening. One such category is the tossing of dice. From the observer's point of view, it is almost impossible to predict the number of dots that will appear when tossed dice cease to move. But, it certainly is possible to predict the outcome that will occur if the simple laws of physics are applied to the throwing of dice. One law states that, "the same cause, operating under the same conditions, will always result in the same effect." You, too, can absolutely determine the desired outcome of rolling dice by operating a knowledge of all forces and actions required to produce the desired result. The result will equal the sum of all forces acting upon it. There is no **chance** involved here. **Chance** has nothing to do with the outcome in dice tossing, the laws of physics are at work.

The right question to ask might be: "Is there any one event exclusive of cause?" For the reality of **chance** to exist there must be, of necessity, the exclusion of cause! The burden of proof is on **chance**. **Chance** must be proven. Cause-and-effect needs no further proof; it has been confirmed unquestionably. (Every time you put two hydrogen atoms together with one oxygen atom you get water. It never misses; no **chance** is involved.) So, to prove the operation of **chance** requires proof for the absence of cause. This has never been accomplished.

No Chance For Chance!

⌘⌘⌘⌘

Science is generally concerned with theories of cause-and-effect but it has little or nothing to say about PURPOSE. However, both cause and purpose are intrinsically built into the operation and structure of the universe and life itself. Without purpose and cause, everything would fall apart and go drifting amidst. Nothing would stay intact. Nothing could keep its identity. Set bounds and limits of activity make life what it is. Set purposes and causes are the sustaining building blocks that make our lives what they are. The parenthetical verses of Colossians 1:16 and 17 not only tell about God's creation of all things in heaven and earth but teaches that it is His purpose and design that holds it all together.

> For by Him were all things created, that are in heaven, and that are in earth, visible and invisible, whether *they* be thrones, or dominions, or principalities, or powers; all things were created by Him, and for Him:
>
> And He is before all things, and by Him all things consist [cohere, are held together].
> Colossians 1:16-17

The Old Testament record of Jeremiah says it beautifully!

> Thus says the Lord, Who gives the sun for a

> light by day and the fixed order of the moon
> and of the stars for a light by night. Who stirs
> up the sea's roaring billows *or* stills the waves
> when they roar – the Lord of host is His name:
> Jeremiah 31:35 (The Amplified Bible)

We humans will always need to answer to a higher power, because man has never created anything. We are not capable of creation in the biblical sense. We are the creation, and we must ultimately answer to the purposes and causes our Creator has designed. Both the broad and specific perimeters of life are God's design.

> Nay, but, O man, who art thou that repliest
> against God? Shall the thing formed say to
> Him that formed *it*, Why hast thou made me
> thus?
>
> Romans 9:20

Plainly, the design of our Creator does not include the operation of **chance**, not even on a microscopic level. Thusly, there is no right response to **chance,** for **chance** does not exist. **Chance** does not fit within the context of purpose. God has built order and harmony throughout the universe. A sheep behaves like a sheep. A duck behaves like a duck. They were created to behave in a precise manner. (Unless, of course, one of them is a so-called "lucky duck.") Our massive planet, Earth, continues to revolve around the sun with just enough tilting back and forth to make our changing seasons an unchanging certainty.

God built order and harmony into the very fabric of life.

No Chance For Chance!

We can count on the constant order and processes that make life work. Sunshine and rain, seedtime and harvest, are a sure constant. Gravity is always there. The air we breathe is always there, praise God! Water to satisfy our thirst is always there. What are the **chances** of all this changing? None! Anyone can see, the concept of **chance** just does not fit into biological and physical spheres of order, harmony, and purpose. Nor does **chance** fit into the functioning of spiritual realties. What a wonderful creation God has made and none of this order is subject to **chance**!

> While the earth remaineth, seedtime and harvest, and cold and heat, and summer and winter, and day and night shall not cease.
>
> Genesis 8:22

⌘⌘⌘⌘

There are exceptions to order and harmony in the universe. The exception to order is disorder. But, these exceptions could be better described as interruptions. Order and harmony normally exist throughout the universe. The oceans stay put within their set boundaries unless an outside force interrupts those boundaries. Interruptions such as tidal waves, volcanic eruptions, tornadoes, earthquakes, and hurricanes change order into disorder. A healthy body is normal; however, disorder changes wholeness into sickness and disease. Often we see these events ascribed to **chance**, but just as often they are described as "acts of God." Both opinions are absolutely wrong. As it has been stated previously, "**chance** is the cause of nothing," and God is not the author of confusion, disaster, or calamity.

> For God is not *the author* of confusion,
> 1 Corinthians 14:33a

God's Son, the Lord Jesus Christ, said of Himself:

> I am come that they might have life, and that they might have *it* more abundantly.
> John 10:10b

God is the giver of life. His will is that we prosper and be in health. He is not the author of sickness, disease, or death. When we are alive and prospering and in good health, we can praise God! We can love Him and thank Him for the blessings He has given us. We are absolutely of no good to God dead! God wants us living and loving and praising Him for all His wonderful works.

God is not the initiator of death, disorder, and destruction. He does not cause catastrophes. But the god of this world does. The god of this world is the devil, and he is the archenemy of the True God. The devil, who is called Satan, is at enmity with God. His plan and purpose is to defeat God's people, God's Word, and ultimately, God Himself. His desire is to elevate himself above the true God so that he is called God Himself. But, he is a thief and a robber. He is the author of death, disorder, and destruction.

No Chance For Chance!

Satan works behind the scenes to accomplish his aims. The secrecy of his moves is designed to defeat the promises of God's Word. As a spirit being, he marshals his powers to intervene and interrupt the order and harmony of God's Creation. Satan is the cause behind disastrous storms and catastrophes. He is the cause behind massive confusion, and he is the force that works destruction and death. But, he is a limited spirit being whose evil workings have been exposed by our Lord, Jesus Christ. We are no longer subject to his devises. Nor should we ever fear his power.

> Ye are of God, little children, and have overcome them: because greater is He that is in you, than he [the devil and his people] that is in the world.
>
> 1 John 4:4

There are those who do not believe spiritual realities exist; therefore, they mistakenly attribute the works of Satan to the preposterous, supposed entity they call **chance**. They mistakenly believe **chance** to be the cause behind massive disasters and destructive events. They attribute **chance** to less spectacular events as well. The natural-minded individual, who does not believe God exists, and who does not believe the devil exists, can and does say **chance** exists. Anemic confessions of **chance** are often the product of a lazy and doubting mind. Those who reject God might believe anything.

⌘⌘⌘⌘

No Such Thing As Luck

There are a few isolated biblical Scriptures where the word **chance** appears. However, no where in God's Word is the concept of **chance** verified. The references, which use the word **chance** or a related word, such as **hap**, actually refer to the following:

Something unexpected	Deut. 23:10, Ruth 2:3, 1 Sam. 20:26, Eccl. 3:19, Eccl. 9:2-3
An occurrence	Eccl. 9:11, 1 Kings 5:4
Accidental; Coincidence; Concurrence	1 Sam. 6:9, Luke 10:13, 1 Cor. 15:37, 1 Cor. 14:10
To meet	Deut. 22:6, 2 Sam. 1:6

6

The one reference in the entire Bible that might appear to verify support for the concept of **chance** is a record concerning the opinion of some pagan, Philistine priests and diviners. (see: 1 Samuel 6:1-12) This record tells how the head leadership of the Philistine nation sought information from these priests. They needed to know what to do with the Ark of the Lord. Since they had captured it from Israel, their whole nation had been plagued. Their priests instructed them to return the ark to its rightful owner, the Nation of Israel, in the following manner:

And take the ark of the Lord, and lay it upon
the cart; and put the jewels of gold, which ye
return Him *for* a trespass offering, in a coffer
by the side thereof; and send it away, that it
may go.

And see, if it goeth up by the way of His own
coast to Bethshemesh [in Israel], *then* He hath
done this great evil: but if not, then we shall
know that it is not His hand that smote us; it
was a **chance** *that* happened to us.

1 Samuel 6:8-9

This phrase, "It was a **chance** that happened to us,"
appears to lend support to the concept of **chance**, but
remember who is doing the speaking here. This reference to
chance is nothing more than the opinion and belief of pagan,
Philistine priests and diviners. This is not God's opinion.
God's Word does not verify **chance**. These priests said that if
the cart carrying the ark does not go to its owner, Israel, then
our trouble is a **chance** happening. Here they were
proclaiming their belief in the possibility of a **chance**
happening. Please note, the oxen took the straight way to
Bethshemesh. According to the logic of these priests, this
was an indication that **chance** was not the cause of their
troubles. And about this they were absolutely right, **chance**
was not the cause of their troubles.

Not much has changed; **chance** often gets the credit for
people's troubles today. It is easy to blame it. It is easy, and
convenient, for some to excuse spiritual realities and, in
unbelief, lay hold upon its false doctrine. The opinions and
theories of men come and go, but the Word of the Lord
endures.

No Such Thing As Luck

> But the word of the Lord endureth for ever. And this is the word which by the gospel is preached unto you.
>
> 1 Peter 1:25

The reason for the omission of the concept of **chance** in the Bible is easy to undertand. God did not design **chance**. The idea of **chance** was invented by the limited minds of ignorant men. It contradicts the truth of God's Word. **Chance** is also antithetical to choice. It is diametrically opposed to it. **Chance** means nothing, but choice has a meaning.

⌘⌘⌘⌘

God's design for life and living leaves nothing to **chance**. What God has built into the fabric of life is choice. We humans are free and rational beings. (Well, we are rational most of the time!) Nevertheless, we have the power of choice built into our capacity. We can be made to do little that is against our willingness. We can choose to love God and believe His Word, which is always profitable to do. We can also choose to deny God and His Word, which is never profitable. We select our beliefs. Whatever we decide to believe, that is what we are going to believe. We can think great thoughts or we can think sordid thoughts; it is up to our personal choice.

In the end, we choose what we think, and we choose what to embrace with our believing action. God designed us with this tremendous ability so that we are capable of choosing to love Him. The first thing that happened was that God chose us.

> According as He [God] hath chosen us in Him
> before the foundation of the world, that we
>
> should be holy and without blame before Him
> in love:
> > Ephesians 1:4

God chose us before the foundation of the world, and we have the personal freedom to respond. The shepherd-king of Israel, David, responded to God's love by declaring:

> I have chosen the way of truth: Thy judgements
> have I laid *before me*.
> > Psalms 119:30

We can choose to love God. We can choose to serve Him and to be thankful unto Him day by day. God made us in such a way that we can have great fellowship with Him. We can respond to His love for us, and God responds to our love and faithfulness to Him.

> And we know that all things work together for
> good to them that love God, to them who are
> called according to His purpose.
> > Romans 8:28

Choice always means responsibility. It is our responsibility and privilege to choose God, to love God, and to believe His Word.

No Such Thing As Luck

> Woe to him who strives with his Maker! – A worthless piece of broken pottery among other pieces equally worthless [and yet presuming to strive with his Maker]! Shall the clay formed say to him who fashions it, What do you think you are making? or, Your work has no handles?
>
> Isaiah 45:9 (Amplified Bible)

You and I may not like to take the responsibility for our choices, but to whom are we going to complain? Complaining is a waste of time. Trying to shift the responsibilities for our choices upon the shoulders of **chance** does not work. We can choose to love God because He first loved us. Why not open up our hearts to God and to His Wonderful, Matchless Word? Why not choose to stand before Him in the righteousness where-with He clothed us in Christ Jesus?

> For the gifts and callings of God are without repentance.
>
> Romans 11:29

⌘⌘⌘⌘

The concept of **chance** seeks to exclude the operation of God and His Word, in our living and our daily lives. It is, however, by His power that we live and move and have our being. Apart from Him and His Word, we have very little.

We can cast the thoughts of our hearts upon Him, for there our hearts will be safe. We can cast our cares upon Him, for He cares for us. Take a look at how the prophet Elisha performed a miracle just for the sake of an embarrassed prophet-friend who had carelessly lost a borrowed ax in the waters of the Jordan River.

> And the man of God [Elisha] said, Where fell it? And he shewed him the place. And he cut down a stick, and cast it in thither; and the iron did swim [float].
>
> Therefore said he, Take *it* up to thee. And he put out his hand, and took it.
>
> 2 Kings 6:6-7

God even cared about this prophet's embarrassment for having lost an ax he had borrowed. In Matthew 10:30, we are informed that God even knows the number of hairs upon our heads. Now that is real individual concern! (Though, for some of us, this requires less counting.)

It is a devilish lie that seeks to limit and exclude God from any category of life. When has God ever removed His power and influence from a single human need? Never, and He never will! The doctrine of **chance** seeks to diminish and belittle God's concern for the individual. But, is there any one phase or function of life about which God has no concern? The answer is, "No!"

> Therefore take no thought, saying, What shall we eat? or, What shall we drink? or, Wherewithal shall we be clothed?

No Such Thing As Luck

> (For after all these things do the Gentiles seek:)
> for your heavenly Father knoweth that ye have
> need of all these things.
>
> Matthew 6:31-32

God has never limited Himself or excluded Himself from the events that affect our lives. Just the opposite is true. God is always there. He is closer than our very breath. People can, and often do, choose to close off their minds to God and choose to exclude God from their lives. But, God is always there for us. He cares what we think, believe, and do. He is concerned about our hearts, our health, and our healing.

Here is a great truth all of us need to understand. Just no category in life is outside of God's care, God's power, and God's love. No matter how big the need you may have, God is big enough to take care of it. No matter how big the failure and sin, God is big enough to cleanse you. No matter how incurable the disease, God is big enough to heal it. No matter how heavy your heart's burden, God's comfort is big enough to make it light. If life looks hopeless to you, God still is big enough. He is the God of Promise and Hope. He is God Almighty! So, what do you need in your life? God is always big enough. God has left nothing to **chance**!

⌘⌘⌘⌘

Now, by having treated the words: **fate, destiny, lot, fortune**, and finally **chance** with a thoughtful examination, the base history of all these terms has come to light. They are all the product of mythological-idolatry. They were bred by idolatry, and mythology was the lying mother that gave them birth. These concepts, and the words by which they are called, have always been bastard children, without legitimacy and without truth. They should never be given any more credence than that which can be found within the context of their idolatrous and mythological homes.

All five of the concepts we studied have developed into full-grown, modern day, living myths. Their legitimacy must be refuted and rejected in our thinking. They tear at the very fabric of our fellowship with our Heavenly Father by contradicting the truth of His Word. We need to do what God's Word says to do and shun these myths and avoid their use. Next, we are going to examine, in more detail, the over-powering influence mythology has upon modern day thinking. We already know that mythological authors defined the doctrinal aspects of "**chance** theologies." We also need to understand how and why these pagan idolatrous concepts continue to live among us today.

No Such Thing As Luck

[1] *Encyclopedia Americana*, Americana Corp., NY, 1962, s.v. "determinism"

[2] Ibid.

[3] *Dictionary of Seventeenth-Century British Philosophers*, Vol. II, Ed., Andrew Pyle, Thoemmes Press, Bristol, 2000, s.v. "determinism"

[4] Pollard, William G., *Chance and Providence*, Charles Scribner's Sons, NY, 1999, p. 136

[5] Greene, Brian, *The Elegant Universe*, W.W. Norton & Co., NY, 1999, p. 136

[6] Young, Robert, *Analytical Concordance to the Bible*, Wm B. Eerdmans Publishing Co., Grand Rapids, MI, 1976, p. 153

The Mythology Express

CHAPTER ELEVEN

The Myth of Mythology

The problem with mythology is that many of its low-minded teachings have spilled over into the realm of what is believed for truth. Because of this, the dividing-line that should differentiate mythology from reality has become blurred. In some realms, the line of separation has been removed altogether. This is especially true of mythology's religious teachings. Its teachings centering on "chance theologies" are thought to be legitimate and truthful aspects of reality. Nothing could be further from the truth.

The religious teachings of mythology have become so interwoven in the fabric of popular thinking that we need to examine the uncanny power they have gained over people's believing. In our study of mythical influence, we first will look at its fictional weirdness. We will see the fuel used to keep it alive and vital. We will also scrutinize how mythical theology is kept before the public. The last aspect of this study will include five biblical records that confront mythical teachings. Hopefully, the reader will discover the tremendous negative influence mythological theologies have produced.

The references to mythology in this chapter refer to its over-all teachings and influence as a body of literature. It is the collective body of mythology that has helped keep individual myths alive. Those who helped collect what we call, "The works of Homer," developed a collective grouping of individual myths. It is this, and other collective groupings, that are today called mythology.

⌘⌘⌘⌘

Much of mythology shows the superstitious, foolish, imaginations of those who authored it. The general thrust of mythical thought also reveals the godless mind-set that has imagined the weird, the absurd, and the ridiculous. We can get a sense of mythic weirdness by taking a short look at the well-known "Creation of the Titans and the Gods" myth.

In this bazaar myth, Gaea, who is called Mother Earth, emerged out of an empty chaos of nothingness. (How did she do that?) Next, without a male partner, she gives birth to Uranus. (This means that somehow she impregnated herself.) Gaea then married Uranus, and he rules over all that comes into being. The first immortal children of Gaea and Uranus, (they were mother and son) were the three, one-hundred-headed giants. Each giant had fifty heads protruding from each arm. (If they were immortal, they would be around today; where are they?)

Their next immortal children were the three Cyclops. Each Cyclops had only one eye, set in the middle of his forehead. [1]

(Hang in there friends, it gets even more bazaar.)

Next, Uranus bound and cast the six children, born to him and Gaea, down into the middle of the Earth. Gaea then hates Uranus and plots his destruction by means of Cronus, one of her next thirteen children. (These children become the first Greek gods.) Cronus strikes Uranus in his genitals, but he, being immortal, did not die. However, from his blood that flowed to Earth, Gaea brought forth a group of hairy-headed giants that had reptile-like feet. Cronus then replaced his father as lord of the sky, but he ignored his promise to Gaea and kept his brothers imprisoned. Gaea then proclaimed that Cronus would one day be overpowered by a son. Trying to stop Gaea's prophecy, Cronus opened his mouth wide and swallowed the first five children born in his marriage to Rhea. Rhea saved their sixth son, Zeus, by hiding him, and in his stead, presented a rock wrapped in a blanket to Cronus. Cronus opened his mouth and swallowed it at once.

Suddenly, Cronus felt an excruciating pain in his stomach. He vomited up the rock, followed by Poseidon, Hades, Hera, Demeter, and Hestia, all of whom were fully grown by now.

Rhea then entered the room, with the young stranger, Zeus, by her side, "Your destiny is upon you, Cronus!" she exclaimed. The Fates prophesied that a son would overpower you

> just as you overpowered your own father. That
> son, Zeus, now stands before you. You are
> reaping the fruits of the seeds you sowed when
> you swallowed our children and kept your
> brothers in chains in Tortarus! [2]

The absurdity of this myth is perfectly clear. Nothing like
this ever happened. This kind of thinking is outside the
bounds of reality; it is unearthly; it is odd; it is errie and
weird.

There is one other creation myth we should look at. The
Prometheus myth gives us its accounting of the creation of
human beings.

> Then down to earth came Prometheus,
> "Forethought," a descendant of the ancient race
> of gods which Zeus had dethroned, a son of
> Iapetus, whom Gaea had borne to Uranus.
> Now Prometheus was crafty and nimble-
> witted. He knew that the seed of heaven lay
> sleeping in the earth, so he scooped up some
> clay, moistened it with water from a river,
> kneaded it this way and that, and shaped it to
> the image of the gods, the lords of the world.
> To give life to his earth-formed figure he took
> both good and evil from the core of many
> animals and locked them in man's breast. He
> had a friend among the immortals, Athene, the
> goddess of wisdom, who marveled at what this
> son of the Titans had created, and she breathed
> the spirit, the divine breath, into his creature
> which as yet, was only half alive. In this way
> the first men were made, and soon they filled
> the far reaches of the earth. [3]

The Myth of Mythology

There are other myths that give different accountings of the creation of man. Just like the above, they are only the man-made, tall tales of their author's imagination. Symmetry, order, and substance are lacking in mythical accounts of creation. They are narratives of events that are outside the range of possibility. There is a noticeable lack of logic throughout all these creation myths.

It is not within the purpose of this book to treat hundreds of myths, but here is a short list of typical, well-known ones. The purpose here is to set forth the imagery projected by the overall theme in each myth's story line.

Title	Authorship	Theme and Imagery
Theogony	Hesiod	The dynasties and creation of the gods and the universe.
The Iliad	Homer	Man's struggle against unrelenting inflexible fate
The Odyssey	Homer	The imaginative tale of human confrontation against monsters, witches, angry gods, and wild creatures.
Olympian II (ode)	Pindar	Songs that honor Greek gods.
Prometheus	Aeschylus	A cunning creator god who wars with other antagonistic gods such as Zeus
Oedipus at Colonus	Sophocles	Humans who are subjected to the laws of Fate.

No Such Thing As Luck

This represents only a minute sampling of early mythological authors. Hundreds of authors have written literally thousands of myths with overall themes and imagery that portray the weird, the absurd, the ridiculous, and even the repulsive. The most casual observer can see that an outstanding characteristic of mythology is its grotesque imagery. The value and soundness of what mythical authorship has produced must be seriously questioned.

⌘⌘⌘⌘

It is by design that the ancient concepts of "chance theologies" are so readily embraced today. These outrageous beliefs have lived through the centuries, and our generation has accepted them with open arms. The process by which these ancient beliefs have continued to remain active through the ages is clearly observable. Mythical authors reflected the rampant idolatry of their day. By their authorship, they assisted in establishing fictitious pagan theologies. Mythical works were established and elevated by successive generations. This is the transportation that delivered fictitious beliefs to the doorsteps of our minds. Without mythology, some other means would be necessary for all of the doctrines related to "chance theology" to have survived. Beliefs about **fate, destiny, lot, fortune,** and **chance** have come directly to us by ancient mythical influence.

For mythical idolatry to travel from one generation to the next it has needed "fuel" to keep it alive and moving.

The Myth of Mythology

(We briefly looked at this process in an earlier chapter, but we need to study it with more depth here.) The "fuel" upon which mythology has traveled is validation. This "fuel of validation" has been generated by authorship recognition. For example, dozens of the renowned authors of ancient literature have referred to the mythological gods of **fate, destiny**, and **fortune**. Succeeding authors have referred to the same gods, and they have quoted the renowned authors for sources of authority. In so doing, they have flattered and validated mythology's authorship. Their quotes have advanced mythical logic by giving credibility to the incredible.

To quote a truthful author and highlight the truthfulness of his words helps truth to live; it helps to keep truth current and alive in the minds of new generations. By the same logic, quoting the dark authorship, that has fostered the outlaw concept of mythological gods and goddesses, promotes idolatrous reasoning and belief. This is the authorship that keeps "luck theology" before the public mind and they have successfully pumped the "life-blood of validation" into the apostate concepts of **fate, fortune, chance**, and **destiny**.

Literary examples that show this validation process abound in the thousands; it would be almost impossible to count them. Just a few brief examples will do for the purpose of this book. The early historian, Herodotus [485 BC- 425 BC] refers to the mythical gods often.

> It is sometimes interesting to see how he makes
> an old myth of the gods come to terms with a
> rational and natural explanation. [4]

Herodotus explains the Thessalians gorge of the Peneus River in the following way. (*Persian Wars, Book VII*):

> The Thessalians tell us that the gorge through which the water escapes was caused by Poseidon, and this is likely enough; at least any man who believes that Poseidon causes earthquakes, and that chasms so produced are his handiwork, would say, upon seeing this rent, that Poseidon did it. [5]

References to mythological gods intervening in human affairs appears over and over again throughout Herodotus' works. (His favorite god might have been Apollo, to whom he refers most often.)

The renowned Plato was born the year after Herodotus died. Plato's works abound with references to the classical Greek gods and to ancient Greek brands of theology. **Fate, destiny, lot, fortune**, and **chance** are qualities and concepts that he describes working in and upon human life. In Book X of the *Republic*, Plato devised his own brand of mythology. In this particular myth, he presents a description of a human soul's pilgrimage. In his narrative, Plato describes the disappointed man whose soul had carelessly chosen the life of tyranny:

> .... he had not made any thorough inspection before he chose, and did not perceive that he was **fated**, among other evils to devour his own children. But when he had time to examine the **Lot**, and saw what was in it he began to beat his breast and lament over his choice, forgetting the proclamation of the prophet; for, instead of throwing the blame of his misfortune on himself, he accused **chance** and the gods, and everything rather than himself. [6]

The Myth of Mythology

Plato may have been a so-called "Great Thinker," but his theology adds up to nothing more than paganism. In the above quote, we see him helping to establish the mythical concepts of **fate, fortune, lot, destiny,** and **chance.** His references to pagan "chance theologies", help in establishing and solidifying these weird ideas. Now, authors have quoted and will continue to esteem Plato's views of **fate,** and **destiny,** and all the other pagan theologies he projected. So, "What is new about that?" you may ask. But this is the very process that has validated mythical teachings; this same process has delivered mythology's teachings to the doorsteps of our minds.

⌘⌘⌘⌘

People today, continue to open their minds and invite mythical teachings into their thinking and believing. A good case-in-point is Wendy Doniger O'Flaherty's book, *Other People's Myths*. In her chapter "Other Peoples Lies," she writes about Plato's attitude concerning myths. The authority of what Plato has to say becomes the springboard by which she jumps into her own, not so private, "swimming pool" of mythological thought. She says of Plato:

> For Plato admits that a myth says something that cannot be said in any other way, that cannot be translated into a logical or even a metaphysical statement. A myth says something that can only be said in a *story*. [7]

237

And now, after having laid the foundation of Plato's authority, upon which she obviously stands, O'Flaherty says of herself:

...which brings me to what I think a myth is. [8]

O'Flaherty can now safely spout forth her teachings that continue to elevate and praise mythology's worth and value.

The last illustration is from a more recent author Brano Leone, who edited the book, *Readings on Homer* (1998). Even before the start of this book, on the book jacket, a spicy quote from Homer's *Iliad* stares the reader in the face. The following is the important impression the book hopes to make on its readers:

> We men are wretched things, and the gods, who have no cares themselves, have woven sorrow into the very pattern of our lives. You know that Zeus, the Thunderer, has two jars standing on the floor of his palace in which he keeps his gifts, the evil in one and the blessings in the other. People who receive from him a mixture of two have varying fortunes, sometimes good and sometimes bad; though when Zeus serves a man from the jar of evil only, he makes him an outcast, who is chased by the gadfly of despair over the face of the earth and goes his way damned by gods and men alike. [9]

So, "the beat goes on"; nothing has changed with the process. Mythology is still quoted and thereby its pagan doctrinal beliefs are substantiated. Validation by authorship recognition continues to "fuel" mythology's uncanny, dubious theology. Plato borrowed and quoted from the myths; and what Plato had to say has been quoted by authors all along in history; and this process is ongoing. It has not stopped. Authors continue to quote Homer, Plato, and all the others they think can add the weight of validity to mythological **fortune, fate, destiny,** and **chance.** They continue to gratify the same ancient pagan beliefs. They continue to glorify the mythical doctrines of pagan idolatry.

⌘⌘⌘⌘

Despite its ridiculous nature, mythological concepts remain popular. Much of the broadcasting media has joined today's God-rejecting authorship, and together they are having a "field-day" of success. They are riding high in their efforts to spread modern day versions of "chance theologies." Because of their efforts, the general public is accustomed to frequent viewings and enactments of mythological imagery.

A good example, which shows how mythology has been blown out of proportion, can be found in the modern day conception of Santa Claus. *Webster's New World Dictionary* defines Santa Claus as follows:

> In *folklore* [unwritten mythology] a fat, white-bearded, jolly old man in a red suit, who lives at the North Pole, makes toys for children, and distributes gifts at Christmas time: [10]

(We would be better off today if the Dutch had kept this myth in Holland.)

No Such Thing As Luck

For decades, the intellectuals who praise the value of mythology and folklore, teach there is a remote resemblance of truth that formed a basis for what has been handed down and believed about Santa Claus. No serious-minded adult, however, would ever accept the reality of our current-day Santa Claus existing in history. Folklore substantiates little, or nothing, about Santa Claus. Old Santa's present day image was developed by the lying imaginations of succeeding generations. Newspaper advertisements, the music recording industry, books and publications, movie theaters, and television programming (especially cartoons), have all helped to foster the mystique of this living and ongoing Santa Claus lie.

Little children are quick to learn that Santa is only the product of deception. They must one day live through their disappointment as they discover the lies. Nevertheless, this mythological character is acted out before children and adults each December, year after year. The effects of this popular myth are not so harmless. The acting out of Christmas mythology shrouds and detracts from the important celebration of the birth of Jesus Christ, who is the Savior of the World.

In the same way that it is not harmless to lie to little children about Santa Claus, it is also not harmless to lie to children who have grown up. Our adult population has been bombarded with lying claims about the general meaning of mythology and folklore. It is certainly not harmless to lie to people about the true meaning of **luck** and **fortune** and **chance**. It is not harmless to call upon **luck** and to embrace it with credibility. It is truthfully a very harmful activity to give credibility to a mythology that is incredible. To do this is akin to calling evil good and good evil. To give credibility to incredible myths is to behave like the Old Testament Judeans who were admonished by the prophet Isaiah:

> Woe unto them that call evil good, and good evil; that put darkness for light, and light for darkness; that put bitter for sweet and sweet for bitter!

> Woe unto *them that are* wise in their own sight!
> Isaiah 5:20-21

⌘⌘⌘⌘

A segment of the intellectual community, along with entertainment producers of movies and television, continue to unduly praise mythology's value. They help to keep outrageous mythologies vital, alive, and common. They do so when they heap their admiration upon mythology as though it were of great value, and even delightful to behold. They do so when they praise its worth and substance, and when they try to make it alluring and charming, entertaining and breath-taking. It is no wonder we hear the general public making uncanny references to "the gods." You might hear these catchy little idolatrous phrases popping up from most any segment of the population: "The gods were smiling on me today."; "The gods were looking down on me."; or "The gods were on my side". It may be hard to believe, but it is true that this kind of ancient mythological, idolatrous thought still abounds in the thinking of our day. The general public is subtly taken in. They are taught to accept mythological logic, and sadly, they are quick to learn its lessons.

Most of us have seen the mythical Hercules and the Cyclops portrayed before us in the movie theater and on television. How old were you when you first saw the larger than life hero Hercules brought to life before your own eyes? And were you ever impressed! Disney produced an animated *Hercules* in 1998. It may have been quite a moneymaker. According to the *2000 Time Almanac*, the movie was rated number two in the top-ten video sales of 1998.

During most of 2001, a Xerox Corporation commercial aired portraying the Greek gods looking down upon the business community here on earth. The commercial was viewed repeatedly by millions throughout that year. While the Xerox Corporation may have been trying to promote their product line and increase their sales volume with this television commercial, that is not all they did. Their portrayal of living, moving, thinking Greek gods, up there in the heavens in their long white robes intervening in the affairs of humans here on earth, effectively helped to keep the mythology of the Greek gods alive and current. They did a "jam-up" job with their presentation. They really made the imagery of mythological gods come-to-life before the public's eyes. The Xerox Corporation is not alone in the promotion of idolatrous mythology. It is heaped upon us today from multiple sources.

The Myth of Mythology

⌘⌘⌘⌘

A community of college and university professors extol the value of mythology and folklore. They are not bashful in setting forth their distorted theories, which supposedly explain what mythology is "really" all about. They teach that mythology reflects the universal human condition; that myths direct us inward; that myths answer who we are and how we should lead our lives. They teach that myths explain the nature of the universe and teach people how to function successfully; that myths explain the nature and function of divinities.

The same secular-minded professionals proclaim, "myths have a serious purpose." A good example of this line of reasoning is set forth in Donna Rosenberg's *World Mythology*:

> Because myths are symbols of human experience, they can be analyzed in a variety of ways depending upon the perspective of the scholar. ...Sigmund Freud and His followers view myths as the expression of the individual's unconscious wishes, fears, and drives. ....Mircea Eliade, views myths as the essence of religion. ..... The anthropologist, Paul Radin, views myths from an economic prospective. ....Carl Jung and his followers, among them, Carl Kerenyi, Erich Neamann, and more broadly, Joseph Campbell, view myths as the expression of a universal collective unconscious. [11]

No Such Thing As Luck

The late Joseph Campbell, who taught at Sarah Lawrence College for thirty-eight years, proclaimed the gospel of mythology's exalted value and relevance to our lives. On the cover jacket to their biography, *A Fire In the Mind*, about Joseph Campbell, Stephen and Robin Larsen have the following to say of Campbell's life:

> Joseph Campbell forged an approach to the study of myth and legend that made ancient traditions and beliefs immediate, relevant, and universal. His teachings and literary works (including *The Hero with a Thousand Faces*, *The Masks of God*, and his immensely popular book of interviews with Bill Moyers, *The Power of Myth*), have shown that beneath the apparent themes of world mythology lies patterns that reveal the ways in which we all may encounter the great mysteries of existence: birth, growth, the development of the soul, death. [12]

Maybe Stephen Larsen intended the above description to be complimentary, but it is not complimentary to those of us who care to look spiritually, and objectively, at Dr. Campbell's interpretations in the field of mythology.

The Larsens, as Campbell's admiring students, sat at his feet. They stood in awe of their professor, and in their biography they heap what is surely an undue, subjective-minded praise upon the man's accomplishments. The same "mythology bug" may have bitten them, which had already bitten their professor Dr. Campbell. Campbell built his reputation by teaching and selling what I would call apostate, twisted interpretations of mythology's meaning and value.

Campbell exposes his blatant opposition to what the Word of God teaches in, *The Power of Myths*. This book consists of his being interviewed by the journalist, Bill Moyers. The interview was taped and has aired occasionally over the years. Here is a small sampling of Dr. Campbell's logic, exemplified in the interview.

> Moyers: Myths are full of the desire for immortality, are they not?

> Campbell: Yes. But when immortality is misunderstood as being an everlasting body, it turns into a clown act, really. On the other hand, when immortality is understood to be identification with that which is of eternity in your own life now, it's something else again. [13]

Please be careful to recognize Campbell, here, makes a mistaken statement that bares the appearance of truth. It is not a misunderstanding that immortality involves an everlasting spiritual body. Those who are born again will receive one at the time of Christ's return to gather his Church. Nor is immortality "identification with that which is of eternity." Immortality is the actualization of living eternally with God; being clothed with and possessing a new spiritual body like the new spiritual body of Jesus Christ.

The truth concerning the particulars of immortality is described in God's Word:

> Now this I say, brethern, that flesh and blood cannot inherit the kingdom of God; neither doth corruption inherit incorruption.

> Behold, I shew you a mystery; We shall not all sleep, but we shall all be changed.
>
> In a moment, in the twinkling of an eye, at the last trump: for the trumpet shall sound, and the dead shall be raised incorruptible, and we shall be changed.
>
> For this corruption must put on incorruption, and this mortal *must* put on immortality.
>
> So when this corruption shall have put on incorruption, and this mortal shall have put on immortality, then shall be brought to pass the saying that is written, Death is swallowed up in victory.
>
> 1 Corinthians 15:50-54

The only "clown act" in this discussion is the "clown act" of Joe Campbell's teaching about the meaning of immortality. What he teaches here stands in blatant contradiction and open defiance of God's Wonderful Word!

Space will not allow us to review all the massive errors propounded in Joe Campbell's interview. However, here is one that is just too hard to pass up.

> Moyers: And yet we all have lived a life that had a purpose. Do you believe that?
>
> Campbell: I don't believe life has a purpose. Life is a lot of protoplasm with an urge to reproduce and continue in being.

Moyers: Not true – not true.

Campbell: Wait a minute. Just sheer life cannot be said to have a purpose, because look at all the different purposes it has all over the place. But each incarnation, you might say, has a potentiality, and the mission of life is to live that potentiality. How do you do it? My answer is, "Follow your bliss." There's something inside you that knows when you're in the center, that knows when you're on the beam or off the beam.[14]

Again, Campbell's mistaken statements bare the appearance of truth. Sheer life absolutely can be said to have a purpose, and there are absolutely no different purposes to life all over the place. The pure, undiluted purpose of all human life is defined in God's Word. That tremendous purpose is fellowship with our loving Heavenly Father. The life of every man and every woman has the potential to love God and to walk with Him and before Him in this life and for eternity. To "follow your bliss," as Campbell recommends, will lead you amiss!

⌘⌘⌘⌘

Our better judgment has been valid all along; the absurdness of mythology is perfectly clear. Nothing like the strange, far-fetched stories of mythology ever really happened.

No Such Thing As Luck

But then came along some smart, supposedly learned intellectuals, who tried to substantiate a "truth meaning" for ridiculous fables and myths. Secular-minded teachers rely on their credentials of scholarship, and the reputations of the universities that employ them, for sources of authority. From their lofty positions of scholarship and renown, they have proclaimed of mythology, "It has a kernel of truth for its source." It is also their "expert opinions" that have determined the lofty value of mythology.

Puffed-up intellectuals have declared that unknown (anonymous) authors of myths were writing metaphorically, symbolically, metaphysically, and even psychosomatically. The same professional scholarship actively continues to teach that it is "the purpose" of mythological authors that make their myths valid and meaningful. They are quick to teach, however, "It is only the practiced eye that can understand and interpret myths properly." Their method reminds me of the devil when he posed a question to Eve in the Garden of Eden:

> Yea, hath God [really] said, Ye shall not eat of every tree of the garden?
>
> Genesis 3:1b

The devil's purpose was to cast a doubt on the integrity of God's Word. And by his subtlety, he beguiled Eve. The scholarship that advances the elevated, "trumped-up" value of mythology, has also tried to cast a doubtful question upon our ability to separate truth from error. Our sound reasoning tells us mythology is unsound in its content, and that it is the literature of fictional make-believe. But, in their subtlety, secular scholars teach there is a "not so obvious meaning" in myths; they say that myths teach "more than is apparent," myths possess "deep meanings." In order to see the not so obvious, you must recognize and use the specialized approach of the reputable professor.

This wayward scholarship proclaims approaches like the metaphoric and the symbolic are required to understand mythological works. Of course, you must always have a professor's particular introduction to the field of study. Thusly, their subtlety has beguiled their students and the public as well. A great many of their conclusions and interpretations stand in direct opposition to the Word of God. They have actually placed their expert opinions above God's Word. Many of them try to belittle God and His Word, and they continue to exalt themselves and their secular-minded teachings. The Christian Community must wake up, see their godless subtlety, and stand against it. The expert's opinions are not always godly opinions; sometimes the expert's opinions are worthless opinions.

⌘⌘⌘⌘

We have paid a huge price for having allowed these puffed-up scholars to teach and establish their godless doctrines in our colleges and universities. They have successfully established their doctrinal errors, and what they have taught has rained down upon our school children. As we have already seen, public school textbooks reflect their sordid doctrines and their expert but godless opinions. The children's sections of our local libraries are well supplied with mythological works. Many of these books are geared with the right language to both seduce and indoctrinate our young children. These works amount to little more than twisted absurdities generated by God-rejecting radical authors. (The small city library, that was surveyed, categorized over sixty juvenile books dealing with the subject of mythology.)

The same small children that read tainted childhood versions of mythology from the libraries, frequently sit before television sets and view cartoon characters which are essentially designed to indoctrinate idolatrous Greek and Roman mythology into their thinking. Mythological characters come to life and live, before their very eyes. They see moving, breathing, animated, life-like Greek gods and goddesses, such as Zeus and Fortuna and the Fates, act out their mythological stories and legions.

The concepts of "luck theology" are introduced to our children at a very young age. A modern day living myth has been helped along by Sue Kueffner's children's book, *Lucky Duck*. The book is designed to be used as a reader for first and second grades. Reader's Digest Children's Books published it, and Wal-Mart marketed it in 2003. Kueffner's little, colorful book portrays the imagery of a helpful yellow toy, Lucky Duck, aiding Emily in her school activities. Emily thinks her little yellow duck is bringing her good **luck**.

The scholarship we are discussing, has developed its own modern brand of mythology, and it can be rightfully termed "myths of mythology." But, their "myths of mythology" are built upon warped scholarship and rejection of Truth. Among other absurd ideas, their "myths of mythology" teaches that the overall text of mythology is a kind of sacred narrative. They reject the rational, and then teach that mythology is not irrational, but rather mysterious and mystical. Another of their myths teaches that ancient myths provide a historical record.

Sadly, arrogant secular scholarship snares and entraps the students who sit in their classrooms. Their "myths of mythology" are designed to make the incredible, credible, and the vain imaginations of men, meaningful. This wayward community of scholarship has been misleading, deceitful, obstinate, and prideful. The preposterous doctrinal errors, which they have fostered, proclaimed, and established, actually amounts to nothing more than useless "myths of mythology."

⌘⌘⌘⌘

This is the right time to dissect mythology and to put it in its proper context. Mythology is fictional writing and belongs in the fictional category. Myths should be viewed as having little or no historical value. They are basically comprised of imaginations that rest outside the bounds of reality; therefore, myths are undependable sources of information. They do not now, nor have they ever had, hidden deep meanings. They are not to be studied with a serious intent to anything. They cannot be studied metaphysically or symbolically, and certainly not psychosomatically. These approaches are anachronistic; they read modern thinking back into the meaning of myths. Myths should be approached as fictional storytelling, on a par with make-believe.

No Such Thing As Luck

This is also the right time to seriously question the credibility and integrity of the authors who wrote ancient myths. Myths are generally the expressions of godless men who project idolatrous views, opinions, and beliefs. Most of their opinions and beliefs are worthless surmisings, which lack soundness and legitimacy. Myths contradict reality and they contradict sound judgment. Generally speaking, mythological authors had no other purpose for writing than that which their narrative reveals. They did not have a subjective motive in writing, nor did their texts have mysterious meanings. What you see, is what you get! Because mythological authors were often pagan God-rejecters, their writings reflect a brand of unsound reasoning, which devised human-like gods, and god-like humans, and animal-like people, popping in and out of the sphere of life.

When it comes to credibility, mythology is its own worst enemy; just read it and see. Don't read what the "experts" say about mythology; just read the mythology and come to your own valid conclusions. Your own personal conclusions will not be much worse, and quite possibly will be better, than the conclusions of those who have claimed a great authority in this category. (As we have seen, a great many of their opinions are way-out in left field.)

The biggest offense of mythology's authorship, and its high-minded, modern proponents is that they both have contradicted God and the Truth of His Word. They stand ardently against the accuracy of what God has proclaimed, going against the grain of what is taught in the Bible. The general thrust of mythology has been a composite of works and tales that were developed by the fantasies of men, fantasies similar to the stupidity of the modern-day Easter Bunny. The authority of what God says in His Word is ignored and countermanded by mythology. It is easy to see that we have two standards at stake. The choice is between truth and error. On the one hand, we have what God has to say in His Word. On the other hand, we have what mythology declares and propounds.

The real issue is that of credibility. Which word is credible: what God has to say or what mythology has to say? There can be no doubt about it. When God, the Creator of the world and all that is therein speaks, it is time to listen. It can only be a prideful, high-minded, self-willed individual who exalts the words of men above the living Word of God. What men say today, they will contradict tomorrow, but God is the faithful God, and His Word is a faithful word. It always comes to pass; it never fails or falters

⌘⌘⌘⌘

Here are a few things that the words of mythology can never do. They can not give you a peaceful heart. Actually, they disturb one's peace! Usually, one's peace of mind goes out the window whenever myths are read. Mythology will never give you rest and understanding. Mythology will never answer your heartfelt question concerning sin and guilt and suffering. Myths will not teach you about healing, forgiveness, and righteousness. Mythology will never show you the love God has for you; nor will it teach you how to get deliverance and wholeness in your life. The man-made fantasies of mythology will never teach you life's greatest victory, which is how to get born-again of God's Spirit; but God's Word does all these wonderful things.

253

No Such Thing As Luck

God's words are peaceful words, and they are easy to be entreated.

> Who *is* a wise man and endued with knowledge among you? Let him shew out of a good conversation his works with meekness of wisdom.
>
> But if ye have bitter envying and strife in your hearts, glory not, and lie not against the truth.
>
> This wisdom descendeth not from above, but *is* earthly, sensual, devilish.
>
> For where envying and strife *is*, there *is* confusion and every evil work.
>
> But the wisdom that is from above is first pure, then peaceable, gentle, *and* easy to be entreated, full of mercy and good fruits, without partiality, and without hypocrisy.
>
> James 3:13-17

God's words bring rest to our souls and hope to our hearts. It is from God's Word that we get understanding. From His Word, we get truthful answers. We get wonderful explanations for all of our heart-felt questions. His Word has solid, concrete answers for all of our needs. His Word abounds with answers, but it also abounds with great promises. It is by our laying a personal claim upon these great promises that we establish the words of God in our lives. God establishes His words and His promises upon every believing heart and mind.

The Myth of Mythology

God's words are vital to our understanding and our prosperity. We need to know exactly what His Word has to say about the subject of myths. There are five scripture references in the New Testament that deal specifically with this matter, and we are going to search them for understanding. The English word, fable, is the Greek word, *muthos*, and should be translated, myth.

> Neither give heed to fables [myths] and endless
> genealogies, which minister questions, rather
> than godly edifying which is in faith: *so do.*
> 1 Timothy 1:4

The context for this instruction is that some in the Ephesian Christian Community of the First Century, were teaching false doctrines that were based upon myths and genealogies. These myths were presented as a genuine source of importance and reference for authority. That myth-based teaching needed to stop. Those involved with this doctrinal error were to be charged (admonished strongly) not to do it any longer. Their myth-based teachings were fostering groundless questions and promoting worthless speculations. The Ephesian believers were not built-up and encouraged by myth-based doctrines; to the contrary, they troubled them. Their quietness and peace was being distracted and disturbed.

The ultimate motive of those who taught mythology in the Ephesian fellowship was to introduce idolatry. The aim of their myth-based doctrine was to cast a doubt by gendering questions that sought to belittle the truthfulness of the Gospel they had been taught. The demonic forces, which push mythology upon us today, are attempting the same devilish work. Their purpose is to introduce idolatry within the Christian Community and to sustain it with a mythological based "chance theology," designed to cast doubts about the power of God and the truth of His Word.

Our second reference is:

> But refuse profane and old wives' fables [myths], and exercise thyself *rather* unto godliness.
>
> 1 Timothy 4:7

Paul was aware of what mythological deception could do. As we saw earlier, he stood on Mars Hill and confronted Greek religion that was based upon mythological gods. Here, he reminds Timothy to stay put on the sound doctrine of God's Word. Even though some in the church had given heed to seducing spirits and doctrines of devils, Timothy is urged to be a good example, standing firmly upon the true doctrine of God's Word. As a youth, Timothy was nourished by the truthful words of his family. He was built up by the sound doctrine of God's Word. Here, he is told to refuse [avoid, or shun] ridiculous, fictional myths.

The best mental diet for Timothy to feed upon was the great Word of God delivered to him at an early age. This is still sound advice for all of God's family. We need to feed our minds upon the good food of God's Word. There is just no time to waste upon the junky trash of what is taught by mythology and expounded by its modern disciples. As we have seen, **fate, fortune, lot, destiny**, and **chance** are all products of what mythology has taught. All of these concepts have developed into full-grown modern day living myths. Their legitimacy must be refused and rejected. We need to do what God's Word says to do and shun them and avoid their use.

Our next reference is:

> This witness is true. Wherefore rebuke them sharply, that they may be sound in the faith;
>
> Not giving heed to Jewish fables [myths], and commandments of men, that turn from the truth.
>
> Titus 1:13-14

Titus was a minister like Timothy. The Apostle Paul left Titus on the Isle of Crete to establish Christian churches there. Titus had his hands full. There was much to do: setting things in order, ordaining elders, and confronting unruly and vain talkers who were deceiving others in the church. These vain talkers within the church were using "Jewish fables" [Jewish myths] almost like authoritative scripture. They themselves had been deceived by unsound myths, and they were attempting to teach them to others in the church. This had to stop. The Christian Believers were distressed. They all needed the clarity of God's Word. God's Word had to become their *only* authority. The mythology had to go; they had to get rid of errors and false mythological doctrines.

The proof of their soundness would be to outgrow the influence of deceiving myths and to lean wholly on the authority of God's Word of Truth. The corrupting influence of mythology was great enough to disrupt early Christian

No Such Thing As Luck

Believers. Left unchecked, that corrupting influence could have devastated their fellowship. Left unchecked, the corrupting influence of mythology is like the rotten apple at the bottom of the barrel, the rottenness spreads. Left unchecked, mythical influence will disrupt sound thought and gender questions of doubt about God and His Word. Left unchecked, mythical influence works to undermine sound doctrine. It will remain a deterrent and an impediment to God's people. It will destroy their peacefulness by troubling their thoughts.

Left unchecked, mythical influence will remain a stumbling block for our youth. They will be "sucked into" adopting a **luck** mentality. They will learn to call upon **good fortune**; and they will use the familiar excuse of **fate** and **destiny**. Their thinking will be based upon the same "**chance theology**" accepted and practiced by the masses of our modern age. We cannot allow this corrupting influence to permeate the thinking of our children. Before we can help them, we must first remove destructive mythical theology from its place of acceptability in our own thinking.

Our next reference is:

> And they shall turn away *their* ears from the
> truth, and shall be turned unto fables [myths].
> 2 Timothy 4:4

This is now the fourth time the Apostle Paul refers to myths. The context for this verse refers to a future day when the Ephesian believers would turn from the sound doctrine of God's Word. The church at Ephesus had been the privileged recipient of the great Apostle Paul's ministry. He had worked personally with them over the years. They had received the tremendous, uplifting, revelation addressed to them in Paul's Epistle to the Ephesian Church. It was by the Christian Believers at Ephesus that the Word of God had sounded-out through all Asia Minor in about a two and one-half year period. Nevertheless, in a future day, these Ephesians were going to desert the Truth they had been taught. They were going to walk away from the accuracy of Truth; and in the place of Truth they were going to adopt fictitious mythical doctrines for their standard of believing and practice.

The Ephesian Church did begin to adopt mythical teachings similar to those of the Gnostic creeds that were contemporarily active around Asia Minor. Like the Gnostics, they began to deny the true humanity of Jesus Christ. Doctrinally, they finally proclaimed Jesus Christ to be God Himself. By under-minding the human capacity and ability of Jesus Christ to walk perfectly before God, the Ephesian Church left the doorway to idolatry open wide. Consequently, they lost the vibrancy and power of the holy spirit that lived within them. This same idolatrous myth that Jesus Christ is God has actively continued since the first century A.D.. Even today, an idolatrous segment in the Christian Community proclaims the man, Jesus Christ, is the God, Jesus Christ. Our wonderful Lord Jesus Christ, however, remains the only begotten Son of God, the Perfect Man.

By embracing the idolatry, that Jesus Christ is God Himself, the church has been robbed of its power and grace today. Many in the Christian Community talk about the power of God, but they show precious little of it in their lives. They have lapsed into "religiosity," which is nothing more than the elusive doctrines of men. The power of God is absent in people's thinking and believing, consequently, leaving a gigantic void. Robbed of the power of God in their lives, people now grasp for straws. They confess "chance theologies" like the power of **fate**, the hand of **destiny**, or the mysterious action of **chance**.

All of this is almost unbelievable, but this is exactly what has happened. The Ephesian Church did not stay put upon the simplicity and accuracy of God's Wonderful Word. They were deceived and led astray. They suffered great personal loss because Satan tricked them. Consequently, the Christian Church has been taken for a miserable ride on a runaway mythology train.

Now is the time for Christians who have been clothed with the power of holy spirit to exit this runaway train. Don't wait for the next stop. Tear-up your tickets and jump off now! Be done with this junky, idolatrous transportation. Start to travel on the accurate roadway of God's rightly divided Word of Truth. Steer clear of the mythical church doctrine that teaches Jesus Christ is God. Dodge the pothole doctrine of **fate** and **fortune**. Start today, walk in the uplifting efficacy and power of our God-given abilities!

The fifth and final reference to the word *muthos* [myths] is:

> For we have not followed cunningly devised fables [myths], when we made known unto you the power and coming of our Lord Jesus Christ, but were eyewitnesses of his majesty.
> 2 Peter 1:16

The basis for Peter's actions, his believing and his preaching, were not built upon myths or mythology. Now, mythology is often cleverly devised; it is sometimes cunningly and authoritatively devised. Peter's teaching of the gospel, however, was not based upon a misleading theology derived from cunningly devised myths. Peter's teaching was authoritative. He had personally heard God say of Jesus Christ, "This is my Beloved Son, in whom I am well pleased." Peter had seen the resurrected Christ Jesus. Peter was born again of God's Spirit. He openly revealed the dynamic power of the holy spirit he had received on the day of Pentecost. He could give forth a word of prophecy. He could heal the sick, cast out devils, and walk and talk with God, even raise the dead. The authority of Peter's teachings was based upon the authority of God's Word. Peter knew God's Word was not the will of men; it was not the words and thoughts of a man. Holy men of God had delivered God's words as they were moved (taught) by God. All of this was the basis for Peter's authority, and the authority of his teaching.

So, what is the basis of our authority today? Surely it is not the outlaw authority of a mythology that teaches the credibility of "chance theology;" the existence of an uncontrollable **fate**; the force of **luck**; the whimsical bestowing of **fortune**, or the riveting confinement of a so-called **destiny**. In the end, the authority of mythology always deceives. It steals and robs sound judgment from those who adhere to it. Mythology's doctrines misguide its followers. It fogs up their clarity of thought, leaving them powerless in understanding, and unfruitful in their living.

The truthful authority of God's Word sets men and women free! Consequently, we are no longer confused about the spiritual forces affecting our lives. God's Word provides great understanding and helps our clarity of thought. We know God's will for our lives because the Word of God is the will of God. This wonderful Word of God has become our basis for sound judgement. It teaches us right precepts. It has taught us how to be born again of God's spirit, and how to openly manifest the presence and power of the holy spirit God has given to us.

By the enlightenment of God's Word, we know how to live life to the fullest. We know how to please God. We know how to bring deliverance to people who call upon us for help. Now we walk by the authority of the name of Jesus Christ. By our own volition, we manifest the awesome authority of God's power and love. God's Word has taught us what is available in this life, and how to receive it – by believing.

> For whatsoever is born of God overcometh the
> world: and this is the victory that overcometh
> the world, even our faith [believing].
>
> 1 John 5:4

---

[1] Rosenberg, Donna, *World Mythology*, Passport Books, Lincolnwood, IL, 1986, p. 6

[2] Ibid., pp. 9-10

[3] Schwab, Gastan, *Gods and Heroes*, Pantheon Books, NY, 1974, pp. 31-32

[4] Lesky, Albin, *A History of Greek Literature*, Thomas Y. Crowell Co., NY, 1966, p. 321

[5] Herodotus, *The Persian Wars, Book VII*, Trans. George Rawlinson, the Modern Library, Random House, Inc., NY, 1942, p. 544

[6] *The Dialogues of Plato*, transl. B. Jowett, Oxford University Press, London, 1953,(Book X 619c) p. 497

[7] O'Flaherty, Wendy Doniger, *Other People's Myths*, MacMillan Pub. Co., NY, 1988, p. 27

[8] Ibid.

[9] *Readings on Homer*, Ed. Brano Leone, Greenhaven Press, San Diego, CA, 1998, book jacket

[10] *Webster's New World Dictionary*, The World Publishing Co., NY, 1968, s.v. "Santa Claus"

[11] Rosenberg, p. Xxi ff.

[12] Larsen, Stephen and Robin, *A Fire In the Mind (The Life of Joseph Campbell)*, Doubleday, NY, 1991, Cover jacket

[13] Joseph Campbell with Bill Moyers, *The Power of Myth* , Doubleday, NY., 1988, p. 229

[14] Ibid.

CHAPTER TWELVE

Luck's Real Meaning

For the sake of accuracy and thoroughness, we are going to take the time to trace a little of **luck's** etymology. There is no need for a long drawn out discussion of its origin because we basically understand the nuts and bolts of what it means already. It should be interesting, however, to follow the road the concept traveled to get into English usage. The most fundamental idea about **luck** matches the theological meaning of **fortune**. The heart of **fortune's** meaning remains "the ability to bestow prosperity." The Romans attributed "the bestowing of prosperity" to Fortuna. Their misguided belief about the ability of Fortuna to bestow prosperity has stayed intact, and traveled to us by two linguistic paths. We are already aware of the path that leads through France. Earlier we saw how the French meaning of **chance** (*cleance*) dropped the meaning of Latin theology. The Old French word **fortune** emphasized unpredictability or **chance**.

No Such Thing As Luck

The other linguistic path **luck** traveled was through the Germanic and Scandinavian languages. The early, Low German word *"luk"*, is closely related to the Modern Dutch *"geluk"*. The prefix *"ge"* is employed in the Middle High German *"gelücke."* This is the source of the modern German *"glück"*, which means good **fortune**.[1] The English dropped the prefix *"g"* and transliterated the German into what is now our word **luck**. Still to this very day, the English word *"luck"* conveys the ancient idea of *"the bestowing of prosperity"* by the power of a god.

⌘⌘⌘⌘

Six chapters of this book have given a full treatment to the common words used in defining **luck**. The fruits of this study have shown **fate, destiny, lot, fortune**, and **chance** to be empty, fictitious concepts. They are worthless ideas that fail to describe anything existing in reality. Rather, they set forth faulty impressions that are derived from pagan idolatrous thought and practice. All of them are theological words, but they are devoid of any real meaning or substance. They refer to powerless gods, falsely perceived. Nevertheless, all of these highly questionable terms are used as trustworthy ideas by our dictionaries, in their effort to define **luck's** true meaning.

Our dictionaries serve us well. Where would we be without them? The men who have labored to provide our English dictionaries deserve our admiration and thankfulness. Though our dictionaries are generally trustworthy, they are far from infallible. When a dictionary defines a given word, that does not close off a discussion of other possibilities and explanations for that word's meanings. As we will see shortly, our dictionary's treatment of **luck** falls short of clarity, and thusly, of accuracy. Our dictionary's focus upon **luck** is myopic; it fails to accurately see **luck** for what it is.

The problem is that the focus of our dictionaries set forth the concept of **luck** without having properly described its illegitimacy. They define **luck** in a manner that presumes it to be a genuinely, reliable idea; a believable reality. It is presented as a word that describes something that truly exists. Each of the words utilized to define and describe **luck** is set forth within a "true-to-reality" frame of reference.

Maybe this is the right time to point out the following: Make-believe gave us fairy tales, and mythology gave us pagan gods, but only truth gives us reality. Bogus concepts and bogus words do not properly define legitimate ideas. The fraudulent concepts of "luck theology" however, do work quite well in defining the inept idea of **luck**. But, by this approach, our dictionaries have succumbed to the faulty standard that utilizes bogus words to define another counterfeit word. They are attempting to report its accepted legitimacy, but they have failed to define its illegitimacy.

So, the authors of our dictionaries have chosen a faulty directional focus for defining **luck**. Their presentation sets it forth to be something that exists in reality. They have said **luck** is something that exists. Next, they have employed the fictitious imagery of "luck theology" to tell us what this something called **luck** is. They have said, whatever **fate, fortune, lot,** and **chance** is, that is what **luck** is. You can plainly see this in *Webster's* definition:

No Such Thing As Luck

> Luck
> 1. The seemingly chance happening of events which affect one; fortune; lot; fate.[2]

The first thing that stands out about this awkward definition is its ambiguous reference to, "the seemingly chance happening of events, which affect one." Obviously, someone has to do the "seeming." So, who is this individual? *Webster's* qualifying phrase in this definition does very little for our understanding; and what is this nasty little reference to the strange word **chance** all about? This is the same kind of subjective language utilized to describe all the **luck** terms we studied earlier. *Webster's* language side steps the most important question; a question that must be confronted. The action of <u>who</u> and <u>what</u> in the definition of **luck** is critical and fundamental information, and must be answered if we are going to know what **luck** really means. Clarity requires that we name the power at work within the concept.

"Chance theology" has been defined consistently by "wishy-washy", weak terminology. There is actually quite a list of ambiguous language associated with each of the words used in defining **luck**. The following is a representative listing of these anemic words and phrases:

> Supposedly, supposed, supposed power, inevitable, something inevitable, that which, happen, a happening, the way things happen, apparent, apparent absence of cause, seemingly fortuitous event, favorable event, necessity, absence of cause.

It is not enough to say of **fate** — it is a supposed power; or of **destiny** — it is the inevitable succession of events; and of **lot** — it is supposedly distributed; and of **chance** —it is an apparent happening; and of **luck** — it is the seemingly **chance** happening of events. What we have with the use of this kind of language is a general lack of clarity. There is just no meat or substance in the above list of words and phrases. They not only fall short of clarity, they are insufficient in naming and identifying causes. Actually, they are purposefully ambiguous. This kind of anemic language fails to answer both <u>who</u> and <u>what</u>, in the action of the word being defined.

By leaving out the identity of who and what, our dictionaries have instead relied upon words that only imply, suggest, or infer the action. These weak words of inference have essentially become "foggy-smoke-screens." They mask the essential and necessary information required for understanding. Why not name the dubious action at work? Why not supply the specific identity of the force supposedly causing the action in the concept of **luck**? Why not say what really needs to be said? There is no profit in being vague and uncertain with the pagan idolatrous thinking represented by this word and the theology it projects. Why not ask honest questions that challenge the truthfulness of **luck**? All the vain, godless, deceitful logic that has produced the strange concepts associated with "chance theologies" also needs challenging. So far, our dictionaries have not met this challenge; they have fallen short.

If **luck** were really a truthful concept, there would be no need to use false imagery to define it. But the authors of our dictionaries have chosen to utilize the untruthful concepts of "chance theology" for its definition. They have done so because there are no legitimate words that can be used in defining a concept that is itself bogus. That is why **luck** fits in so perfectly with all the deceptive terms consistently used in its definition. Words that are equal to the same thing are equal to each other. Likes attract one another, even in the category of word definitions; yes, especially in the category of word definitions. This is the true reason why **fate, lot, fortune**, and **chance** have been drawn into the definition of **luck**.

Take away the phony concepts of "chance theology" and the word **luck** has absolutely no foundation upon which it can stand. It crumbles in sinking sand. This is **luck's** rightful place, because it is a concept without a genuine foundation. Without a legitimate foundation, it becomes just a meaningless, misleading, empty idea; this is what it has been from its inception. There are actually no words to validate **luck** except to say it just does not exist; that it is an unreal and invalid idea. There is no such thing as **luck**!

⌘⌘⌘⌘

The fundamental arguments for the idea of **luck** are not new, nor have these arguments changed through the ages. Throughout the pages of this book, we have confronted these long-standing, controversial arguments head-on. Now that the deceptive mask projected by the concept of **luck** has been removed, we can see its alarming identity. Its uncanny weirdness is outrageous. In the last pages of this work, we need to "snuff out" any life remaining in the worthless meaning of this word. We also need to bury, and put to rest, all of the far-fetched, ridiculous claims of "luck theology." We cannot allow the image of **luck's** meaning to linger in our thinking and "fog up" the clarity of our reasoning. What we need is a firm, straightforward, accurate understanding of both what **luck** is and what it is not. The following condensed presentation of **luck's** true meaning should be helpful. First, we are going to see what **luck** is <u>not</u>.

> **Luck is <u>not</u> fate, fortune, lot, destiny,** or **chance.**

It is none of these things. All of these concepts are outgrowths of pagan idolatry. They describe the meaningless qualities and attributes of false pagan gods. All these fictitious concepts were conceived by idolatrous minds and have been nurtured and personified by the fictional literature of mythical authors. Though these deviant terms are used extensively today, they represent bogus concepts that describe nothing existing in reality. These words cannot rightfully define **luck.**

> **Luck is <u>not</u> a natural impulse,** nor does it operate through personal instinct.

There are some that make the claim that **luck** leads them by impulse or instinct. This cannot be true! Animals are guided by what we call instinct. Humans are basically guided by understanding and discernment. Our state of consciousness emanates from habit patterns and learned responses. It is also true that we have survival instincts and emotional instincts. People do have natural inclinations and abilities – all of this is true. However, **luck** cannot operate through a gifted instinct because it cannot operate period! It cannot guide men to success. Those who lay a claim to gifted sensory perception and magical insight are duplicating the claim of the "false priests" we studied in Chapter Seven. Spiritual abilities come with our new birth; they are God-given. Devil spirits guide people by possession. They can control a human mind by manipulation.

> **Luck** is <u>not</u> an inexplicable force that cannot
> be understood, explained, or accounted for.

It is certainly true that there are many things that are not understood in life, but **luck** is not one of them. The superstitious beliefs that are taught about a "luck-force" existing beyond human knowledge and comprehension add up to nothing more than groundless, off-beat speculation. The natural-minded, irrational man has imagined the existence of a force called **luck**, and then says, "It can't be explained." So the non-existent, but popular imagined force of **luck** has developed into a catchall explanation for good and evil. But, the only forthright and truthful explanation for the forces of good and evil are clearly spelled out in God's Word. There are no other spiritual forces affecting our lives, beyond those that are thoroughly explained by God's Word.

> **Luck** is <u>not</u> an innocent, harmless, crutch-word
> that can be used without any real impact or
> consequences.

It is not a harmless activity to contradict God and the truth of His Word. God promises in His Word that He is the legitimate and genuine bestower of blessings and benefits, and that true prosperity comes by Him alone. To rob God of

His praise and give it to a **luck** god is not a harmless activity. It is first and foremost idolatry! If using the word **luck** is a habit, it is a harmful habit that needs correcting. The acceptance of this word starts in the heart. If we love God with all our heart, there is just no room left for doubtful reasoning about **luck**. The implications of employing and using the word **luck** to explain this or that, are far-reaching. The impact of its use is to speak forth a devilish lie designed to cast a doubt upon the true source and supplier of blessings and benefits – God, our Heavenly Father. Even to use it in jest fortifies the same lie.

> **Luck** is <u>not</u> a source of prosperity, nor is it the cause of evil and destruction.

Early in their existence, men denied God and His Word. They began to devise their own explanations and beliefs about the causes of prosperity and destruction. Eventually, in Roman times, men attributed prosperity to a goddess named Fortuna. Today, the goddess Fortuna is called **Luck** and people continue to foolishly and mistakenly credit it with the power to bestow prosperity. The true and abiding source of prosperity is God, the Creator of heaven and earth. He alone is the Giver of Life. The blessings we enjoy in life are from Him. We cannot allow misguided teachings about the power of **luck** to trick us out of our abiding expectations of God and His Word. We need to love and praise God more and more each day, for He is surely our bountiful supply, and it is He that keeps us safe from harm. The archenemy of God, called the devil and Satan, is the source of evil, destruction, and death.

No Such Thing As Luck

Luck is <u>not</u> a creation of God.

The idea of **luck** is a man-made concept that stands in opposition to God. God never created a vacuum or sphere of activity outside, or exempt from, the reach of His power and love. There is no place in the universe where the power of **luck** operates. The only place in which the false and powerless concept of **luck** maintains a seeming legitimacy is between the ears of a God-rejecting human mind, one that has imagined vain things.

Luck is <u>not</u> a characteristic factor that defines our human condition.

The doctrinal perspective that teaches **luck** happens, without any obvious rational, and that all humans are subject to it, is a misguided belief. Teaching of this sort offers a narrow, limited conclusion that fails to comprehend spiritual realities. It is from a purely, five senses, natural-minded perspective, that men have worshipped idols and embraced superstitions. Their limited knowledge fails to detect the operation of devil spirits, which are drawn to idolatrous practices. It is from this natural-minded prespective that a definition of **luck** sprang forth. As stated again and again, valid understanding and discernment must include a spiritual perspective. It is from a spiritual perspective that we can discern many of the commonly misunderstood causes operating both in and upon life. Spiritual understanding clears up the muddled shadows of human doubt about the causes and effects operating in this world and in our lives individually. The spiritual light of God's Word enlightens our lives. It enables us to live our lives with understanding, success, and confidence. Discerning of spirits is a God-given ability that came with our new-birth. Every man and woman born of God's spirit has the capacity to manifest this ability when they are taught how to do so! Because of our spiritual ability, we are no longer subject to the prince of the power of the air and the host of his evil spirits. Devil spirits flee when they are commanded to do so in the powerful name of Jesus Christ, our Lord, and Savior.

> For the Lord giveth wisdom: out of His mouth cometh knowledge and understanding.
> Proverbs 2:6

Luck is <u>not</u> accident, happenstance, or circumstance.

The word accident is generally used in reference to an event that is not expected, foreseen, or intended. But the origin of this word comes from the Latin *cadere*, meaning to fall, as to fall out. As we learned earlier, *cadere* was a theological term referring to that which false Roman gods were believed to shed forth upon individuals. Although unexpected, unforeseen and unintended events do occur, these events have nothing to do with the force of a Roman god, nor the modern "luck god." Spiritual manipulation by Satan and his devices does influence what many times appears to be an accidental event. People also influence so-called accidents with careless behavior, narrow-minded vision, and thoughtlessness.

Happenstance originally referred to a befalling - to that which was going to happen by the word or action of a god. There being no way to know what the god was going to do, the future outcome became a matter of **chance**. So, **chance** is the bottom line definition for happenstance; the same theology that generated the word accident also generated happenstance. In content, they have the same meaning. The English version is happenstance; the French version is accident, or *accidens* – to fall.

Circumstance refers to cause. For example: what are the causes resulting in an event? *Webster* defines it as follows:

> A fact or event accompanying another fact or event, either incidentally or as an essential condition or determining factor. [3]

Luck is never an essential condition or a determining factor for any event, because it has no power to act upon anything.

> **Luck** is <u>not</u> a force that comes and goes in cycles.

This common, but misguided teaching sets forth the idea that **luck** changes in cycles. If you are having good **luck** now, that will change and if you are having bad **luck** now, that will eventually change too. The false science of astrology is built upon this belief. Astrology teaches that changing positions of heavenly bodies affects our lives. Others place their believing on **lucky** days and **lucky** numbers. All of this "fortunate-cycle mentality" ultimately leads to emptiness, longing, and despair. It is a hoax! **Luck** remains a powerless force, and works neither good nor evil, this day or any other day. The prophet Jeremiah warned God's people not to fear the gods of the heathen, nor to participate in pagan logic.

> Thus saith the Lord, Learn not the way of the heathen, and be not dismayed at the signs of heaven; for the heathen are dismayed at them.

For the customs of the people are vain: for *one* cutteth a tree out of the forest, the work of the hands of the workman, with the axe.

They deck it with silver and with gold; they fasten it with nails and with hammers, that it move not.

They are upright as the palm tree, but speak not: they must needs be borne, because they cannot go. Be not afraid of them [heathen luck gods], for they cannot do evil, neither also *is it* in them to do good.

Jeremiah 10:2-5

⌘⌘⌘⌘

Now that we have established what **luck** is <u>not</u>, finally we can move ahead with certainty and accurately name what **luck** is, and what it has been, throughout its sordid history.

Luck is a religious devotion.

Those who embrace its meaning, sing its praises. They pay it homage. They bow to it within the depths of their hearts and minds, seeking its blessing and summoning its protection from harm's way. They believe in **luck's** power and they attribute its works to many categories of life. Their outstanding confessions, and the manner in which they embrace **luck**, certainly is a religious devotion. In fact, and in practice, this is exactly what the underlying reality of this word is all about. The concept of **luck** stands for the characteristics of a god. A confession of **luck** is a religious acknowledgement of one's belief in the power of that god. When an individual continues to confess **luck**'s reality, that individual is expressing his, or her, religious devotion.

Luck is an idolatrous confession.

It blatantly denies what God has proclaimed of Himself by His Word. God promises in His Word that He is the giver of prosperity and safety. To confess a belief in **luck** is to take a stand in direct opposition to God and what He has promised. In affect, it is calling God a liar by negating His Word. The word **luck** is itself an attempt to call idolatry by another name. The idolatrous action of this word is that it attributes the work of God's hand of blessing to a false god – it names a god called **luck** to be the power that supplies. The idolatrous confession of **luck** attempts to cast off God and His Word, and then proclaims, "**Luck** is truth; **luck** is real, and it lives!" But, **luck** is only an idol that has been erected within a human's mind; it remains the idolatrous confession of an idolatrous heart and mind.

> For God hath not given us the spirit of fear;
> but of power, and of love, and of a sound mind.
> 2 Timothy 1:7

Luck is a corruption of sound thought and will.

It was after Adam lost his spiritual connection with God that the sound thinking of men and women started to corrupt. The foolish reasoning of natural-minded men sought to elevate their thinking above God's Word. The evil conclusions of godless men attributed prosperity and safety to idolatrous gods - gods they had imagined and made with the works of their own hands. Their corrupted theology ascribed power to objects that had no power. God-rejecters elevated and praised the false concepts of **fortune** and **fate** and **destiny**. They replaced truth and in its place, they established a foundation of errors. Their unprincipled, reprobate surmising replaced the bedrock certainty of God's Word of Truth with the sinking sand reasoning of "chance theology." Today people call this same unfounded reasoning by a new name — they call it **luck**.

Luck is a misguided belief in the existence of a metaphysical god.

The supposed god of **luck** is mysteriously hidden from view; nevertheless, many believe it is a generating force causing good, and working evil. Although there is no physical semblance to see or touch, active belief in this metaphysical god continues. Popular belief in **luck** is kept alive by the metaphysical teachings of mythology. This bewildering body of metaphysical theology has been elevated to a place almost like Scripture. These legendary, "scripture-like" records have captivated people's believing. They depict the defining qualities of what **luck** is. It is the acceptance of these mythological teachings, and the images they project, to which people bow in their hearts. It is to the unsound, idolatrous images of "luck theology" that they give homage. **Luck** has become the modern embodiment of these ancient metaphysical theologies, and it is to this metaphysical **luck** god that people kneel with reverence in their thinking and believing.

Luck is a denial of cause and effect.

Often, people try to shift their responsibilities. But, the free-will choices we make either make or break us. We live or die by our choices. When a man calls upon the power of **luck** to add riches and fame to his life, he is going to be disappointed, because it is only an empty illusion. On the other hand, when a man calls upon God to prosper his way, and opens up his hands to receive that prosperity, God is going to fill his hands to overflowing. God is the cause of blessings. A believing heart that is prepared to receive procures His blessings. Simply put, we receive what God has promised by believing to receive it. There are no ifs - ands - or - buts about it; what God has promised in His Word always comes to pass. His promises are to us and they are fully available for us to receive. He alone is the cause of our blessings. A confession of **luck** is to deny the real cause of any blessing. The effect of such a denial is empty hands, empty pockets, and ultimately a disappointed, empty heart.

A confession of luck is passive submission to fatalistic thinking.

Fate and freedom stand in direct opposition to one another. **Fate** is mistakenly called a force that can lock an individual in, and take away freedom of choice. Whether for good or bad, an individual must accept what is beyond his power to resist. He must also accept his lack of ability to appropriate, or generate, prosperity. This is the exact place "luck thinking" carries men and women. Their dependency is locked into the ability and power which **luck** is proclaimed to have. Their energies and efforts are tied up. They wait and wait; what else can they do? If they are going to be blessed, or protected, it will be at **luck's** option and not their own. Maybe it is high time for people of this persuasion to wake up and take a serious look at the dooms-day god they are waiting upon! The True God does not delight in our waiting around for His blessings. They are available right now – daily. What all of us needs to see and understand is just how far-reaching God's love goes. His love has given us a freedom to choose and act according to our personal believing and judgment.

Luck is a doctrine of devils; it stands diametrically opposed to the Word of God.

The design of "luck theology" is purposefully crafted to question and refute the abiding reality of God and the sure promises of His Word. Demented teachings about **luck** seek to rob God of the praise and honor He is due. The lying doctrines surrounding the idea of **luck** claim that it is the source of prosperity and protection. When an unexpected blessing comes, the power of **luck** is credited. Those who subscribe to this belief rob God of the praise He is due. To confess **luck** is to deny God. It is to deny His love and His benefits. It is to turn one's back on God and give the praise that belongs to Him to a false metaphysical entity. To embrace **luck** is to embrace a doctrine devised and elevated by devilish influence and intent.

No Such Thing As Luck

The following is a three sentence, concise, "nutshell" summation for the meaning of **luck**.

> ◆ **Luck** is a religious devotion, an idolatrous confession, a corruption of sound thought and will. It is a misguided belief in the existence of a metaphysical god; a denial of cause and effect. **Luck** is passive submission to fatalistic thinking; a doctrine of devils that stands diametrically opposed to the Word of God. ◆

Not exactly the dictionary's definition, but free from cloudiness. It paints a clear picture. It accurately points out truth and exposes error.

We are surely going to remove the use of this word **luck** from our normal vocabulary. But, what are we going to replace it with, now that we no longer bid people "good luck"? What are we going to say instead? How about some uplifting words that offer encouragement and inspiration! Replace what were empty, meaningless words with the positive assertion: "You can do it, give it your best, or try your hardest, or may the better team win." What could be more wonderful than the encouraging prayer, "God's blessing upon your undertaking."? It is as simple as looking at the truthfulness of what needs to be said and saying it. That is going to work every time.

Uncanny references to "How **fortunate** I am," can be replaced by, "How blessed I am" or "God has blessed me abundantly." Replace abstract talk of **chance** with enlightened references to the actions of spiritual forces, and cause and effect realities. Jesus Christ addressed the serious

282

consequences of what we choose to say.

> But I say unto you, That every idle word that men shall speak, they shall give account thereof in the day of judgment.
>
> For by thy words thou shalt be justified and by thy words thou shalt be condemned.
>
> Matthew 12:36-37

The far-reaching significance of our words influence men and women; loving words of truth set them free.

⌘⌘⌘⌘

Without the ability to separate truth from error, men and women grope and stumble in darkness. They may boast of outstanding accomplishments, and of knowledge and wisdom; however, they still end up adopting flaky man-made standards which lead them astray. They lack soundness, purpose, and direction. Often, they barely know which end is up!

> The thoughtless, the ignorant, and the indolent, seeing only the apparent effects of things and not the things themselves, talk of luck, of fortune, and chance. Seeing a man grow rich, they say, "How lucky he is!" Observing another become intellectual, they

exclaim, "How highly favored he is!" And noting the saintly character and wide influence of another, they remark, "How chance aids him at every turn!" They do not see the trials and failures and struggles which these men have voluntarily encountered in order to gain their experience; have no knowledge of the sacrifices they have made, of the undaunted efforts they have put forth, of the faith they have exercised, that they might overcome the apparently insurmountable, and realize the Vision of their heart. They do not know the darkness and the heartaches; they only see the light and joy, and call it "luck"; do not see the long and arduous journey, but only behold the pleasant goal, and call it "good fortune"; do not understand the process, but only perceive the result, and call it "chance." [4]

The "enticing words of man's wisdom" are crowded with errors that delude. [5] They are based upon the logic of idolatrous speculation, superstition, mythological imagery, and the inflated ego of human logic. A great many of these "enticing words" can be found in the high-sounding philosophies of scientific theories and man-made religious creeds and theologies. The "enticing words of man's wisdom" have given us the "luck theologies" of **fate, destiny, lot, fortune,** and **chance**, but human wisdom betrays us. Earth bound wisdom has given us deceptive explanations for the great realities of God. The wisdom of this world is based upon the soundest judgements men are capable of declaring, but the wisdom of this world pales before God.

Where is the wise man (the philosopher)?

Luck's Real Meaning

> Where is the scribe (the scholar)? Where is
> the investigator (the logician, the debater) of
> this present time *and* age? Has not God shown
> up the nonsense *and* the folly of this world's
> wisdom?
>
> 1 Corinthians 1:20 (The Amplified Bible)

The enormous controversy surrounding **luck** must be completely resolved in our hearts. We need humble hearts to receive what God has to say. Meekness to God's Word is the key attitude we must maintain. We are not among the critics who choose to question God's Word. Rather, to the contrary, we are persuaded that "God is not a man that He should lie." What He says, "is!" We know this is true because He is the Creator. He is the sustainer of life and we are His creation. We answer to God, and He will never answer to us! God is the ultimate authority, and the accuracy of His Word is unquestionable. It has stood the test of time, and it will stand the test of eternity.

We can safely trust our Heavenly Father to do what He says He will do. We can steadfastly base our believing upon the promises of His Word, because they always come to pass. We cannot lean upon our limited understanding because we honestly do not have the capacity within ourselves to answer the critical questions of life and eternity. Most of the time, we don't even know the right question to ask. This world's wisdom is temporal and fleeting. The words of men are often crafted in cleverness to deceive. Why would we ever embrace the conflicting words and doctrines of man-made "luck theologies" above the Word of God? There is no sanity in such a choice.

No Such Thing As Luck

Earlier in Chapter Two, we saw how men of corrupt minds "suppressed the truth" of God's Word. They had no excuse for their behavior, because they denied the plain and evident reality of God's power and glory. We also saw how they became vain in their imaginations. They claimed to be wise, but they were fools. They had exchanged the glory of God for their own worthless, man-made images. They literally denied the power and glory of God. Defiantly, they proclaimed that the gods they had made were the true source of power and glory, but they proclaimed a lie! The course of their actions has continued to draw and persuade men and women. The worthless images they vainly sought to empower remain active among us. The idolatrous concepts of **luck** and **lot, fate** and **fortune**, along with a host of other worthless images, are as popular today as they have been all along in history. These long-standing lying images remain appealing to millions who readily embrace them. That needs to change!

The unwise course of God-rejection continues in our day. People who choose to deny God's Word and His Power, continue to rely upon images they themselves have imagined. Within their God-rejecting minds, they defiantly set forth that the ancient, false, worthless images of "luck theology" are truthful and powerful. Thusly, they substantiate the identical lie set forth earlier by the corrupted men described in the book of Romans. Like the corrupted men of early history, God-rejecters today become "vain in their imaginations and their foolish hearts are darkened." The lies they utter never change.

> The thing that hath been, it *is that* which shall be; and that which is done *is that* which shall be done: and *there is* no new *thing* under the sun.

> Is there *any* thing whereof it may be said, See,
> this *is* new? it hath been already of old time,
> which was before us.
>
> Ecclesiastes 1:9-10

Men today, continue to "hold the truth" of God's Word in unrighteousness. They continue to construe and to promote the ancient, corruptible images of "luck theologies"; they continue to rebel against God's Word. But we are not among them, for we are born again of God's spirit.

Men and women will live without spiritual ability and perception, until they are born again of God's spirit. Because God is Spirit people need a spiritual connection in order to communicate with Him. God knew we would need to have a spiritual rebirth in order to be born of His spirit. The new birth is the greatest of all blessings! The greatest blessing in all of life happens when anyone believes God raised His Son Jesus Christ from the dead and deliberately decides to make Jesus Christ the Lord of their life. Whenever this happens, they become born again of God's spirit. God has built a longing for eternity into the human heart, and He has made eternity fully reachable by our spiritual rebirth. It is by our spiritual birth that we gain spiritual power and ability. The spirit-life, which now lives within us, enables and empowers us. Now we are sons and daughters of God; we are no longer a body and soul creation. We are now men and women of body, soul, and spirit. We have a spiritual connection with God. We can walk and talk with God, and He abides with us. God teaches us by the spirit we received from Him.

> Now we have received, not the spirit of the
> world, but the spirit which is of God; that we

might know the things that are freely given to
us of God.

Which things also we speak, not in the words
which man's wisdom teacheth, but which the
Holy Ghost [Holy Spirit] teacheth; comparing
spiritual things with spiritual.

1 Corinthians 2:12-13

The ability to separate truth from error is essential to every
Christian Believer's life and walk. We have that ability by
virtue of our new birth. Now we must absolutely walk and
live by openly manifesting the power God has given to us.
The essentials, concerning truth and error, are clearly stated
in God's Word and we can live confidently by that Word!

O taste and see that the Lord is good: Blessed
is the man *that* trusteth in Him.

Psalms 34:8

If we are going to steer clear of trouble and enjoy prosperity,
we must know all the forces operating about our lives. Never
are we to get sidetracked by the deceitful doctrines of men,
nor by Satan's devilish doctrines. Both are designed to trick
us. We keep our hearts fixed upon God and His Word. We
listen to God as He directs our steps, and we maintain a
thankful attitude by a thankful heart!

To move away from the trash can confessions of "luck
theology" is a must! There is no further need to bring **luck**
into our thinking; it has no pertinence because it has never
been a living entity. Any validity this concept may have

occupied in our thinking has surely been buried and laid to rest. We need to direct our thoughts to the spiritual causes of events. Our believing must be centered upon God and His Word.

When God's hand of blessing is bestowed upon our lives, we need to say so, emphatically. We need to look up and say, "This blessing is the work of God, my Heavenly Father. He has prospered my life." Our natural response should be to stand before God with thankful hearts and acknowledge Him with the honor and praise He is due. Whenever disorder, destruction, and death are about us, we must recognize the source of this also. By doing so we can stand against any of these devilish works.

> Submit yourselves therefore to God. Resist the
> devil, and he will flee from you.
>
> James 4:7

A few years ago, my wife discovered that she had developed breast cancer. She did not come to me and say, "Wow, Honey, what bad **luck** I have!" Instead, we recognized this attack of the devil for what it was, an attempt to take her life. God's Word has taught us,

> Many *are* the afflictions of the righteous: but
> the Lord delivereth him out of them all.
>
> Psalms 34:19

She claimed this promise from God's Word and the deliverance came. She is cancer-free. Wow, what good **luck**! NO! Praise God!

289

No Such Thing As Luck

By embracing the sound judgements of God's Word, we establish truth in our thinking. The latent potential of God's Word is absolute. It works effectually in us, and for us, as we believe it. It is our believing that appropriates what God has declared by His Word. Whenever men and women get fully persuaded about the promises God has made to them, they are going to see great promises come to pass. Our believing fully meets the requirement. It is by our believing God that we prosper.

> But without faith [believing God] *it is* impossible to please *Him*: for he that cometh to God must believe that He is, and that He is a rewarder of them that diligently seek Him.
>
> Hebrews 11:6

God is always the faithful rewarder of those who seek Him out with all their heart. It is our confidence, conviction, reverence and obedience, which are testaments to what we believe about God. Believing God's Word has always been the action required of us!

To believe God's Word means that we seek after His Word. We diligently seek it out, because it never fails us, it never lets us down. We can always count on it, day and night. We carefully rely upon its judgments, its wisdom and understanding, its values and validity. This is how God's Word becomes the foundation for our actions in life. It motivates us and it directs our paths. It teaches us what to believe, and it corrects our believing when it gets out of line.

It is easy to get excited about God's Word because it enriches us with the light of life. It enables us to walk successfully through the darkness of this world. As we look to God, He always supplies. He never lets us down.

290

Luck's Real Meaning

Blessed *are* they which do hunger and thirst after righteousness: for they shall be filled.

Matthew 5:6

The simple but sure key to God's abundant blessings is to prove Him in our lives. We acknowledge God by believing His Word. We thank Him for His abundant blessings in our lives; and we love and praise Him. Then, we open our hands to receive the abundant blessing God has promised.

⌘⌘⌘⌘

It is true that in our day there is very little opposition to worthless teachings and beliefs that center around **luck, fate, destiny, lot, fortune**, and **chance.** Those who use these words, and teach their precepts, spout forth their opinions; rarely are they challenged. They have had free reign. But this is the right time for Christian Believers to confront the empty doctrines that have been cast before us. Now is the right time for us to elevate our thinking and be done with these worthless concepts! Now is also the right time for people everywhere to rise up with thoughtful minds and thankful hearts to give God His rightful praise! It is He who has blessed us, watched over us to prosper our lives, and kept us safe from harm.

The next time a good intentioned friend or acquaintance wishes you "good **luck**", be ready. Tell them you had rather have their heartfelt prayers. Tell them how you look to your Heavenly Father for His blessings upon the activities of your

No Such Thing As Luck

life. Let them know it is God who enriches and protects. Let them know that confessing **luck** is just a modern day form of idolatry. Teach them to count on God. God is always faithful to His Word.

As "**luck** would have it" is no longer available; it is no longer a viable option. **Luck** has had its day and that day has ended. It has been buried and laid to rest. All of us can now say, with tremendous authority, "**There is no such thing as luck!**"

[1] Ayto, John, *Arcade Dictionary of Word Origins,* Arcade Pub., N.Y. 1991, s.v. "luck"

[2] *Webster's New World Dictionary,* The World Publishing Co., NY, 1968, s.v. "luck"

[3] Ibid., s.v. "circumstance"

[4] Allen, James, *As a Man Thinketh,* Fleming H. Revell, a division of Baker Book House, Grand Rapids, MI, p. 58

[5] 1 Corinthians 2

Scripture Index

Genesis

1:28	175
3:1b	248
8:22	215
10:8-9	47
12:1-2	55
12:2-3	175
30:10-11	57
31:29-30	57

Exodus

8:25-26	60
32:7-8	61

Deuteronomy

18:10	146
18:20-22	153
22:6	218
23:10	218

Joshua

11:17	65
12:7	65

Ruth

2:3	218

1 Samuel

6:1-12	218
6:8-9	219
6:9	218
20:26	218
30:7-8	152
30:18-19	152

2 Samuel

1:6	218

1 Kings

5:4	218
18:21	133
18:24	134
18:36b-37	135
18:38-39	135
22:10-12	143

2 Kings

6:6-7	223
17:16-18	66

Psalms

1:3	38
14:1a	101
34:8	288
34:19	289
37:4	136
95:1-3	177
96:4-5	120

106:19-20	61
115:4-8	104
119:30	221

Proverbs

| 2:6 | 275 |

Ecclesiastes

1:9-10	286
3:19	218
9:2-3	218
9:11	218

Isaiah

5:20-21	241
45:9	222
52:4	58
65:11	64

Jeremiah

10:2-5	276
10:14-15	148
31:35	214
44:17	66
44:22-23	67
50:2	49
51:44	49

Amos

| 5:25-26 | 63 |

Malachi

| 3:10 | 37 |

Matthew

5:6	291
5:45b	176
6:31-32	224
10:30	223
12:36-37	283
12:37	112
15:18	112

Mark

| 11:23-24 | 166 |

Luke

| 10:13 | 218 |

John

4:24	109
10:10a	109
10:10b	216

Acts

14:8-12	80
14:14-15	82
17:16-21	83
17:22-23	85
19:27	77

Romans

1:20-23	43
8:28	221
9:20	214
10:9-10	133
11:29	222

1 Corinthians

1:20	284
1:21	85
1:22-23	73
2:12-13	287
2:14	106
14:10	218
14:33a	216
15:37	218
15:50-54	246

2 Corinthians

4:3-4	109

Ephesians

1:3	176
1:4	221
1:4-5	131
4:14	68
4:15	68

Philippians

4:13	130
4:19	38

Colossians

1:16-17	213

1 Thessalonians

1:9b	88
2:13	150

1 Timothy

1:4	14, 255
4:7	256

2 Timothy

1:7	278
2:15	149
4:4	258

Titus

1:13-14	257

Hebrews

11:6	290

James

1:17	175
3:13-17	254
4:7	289

1 Peter
1:25   220

2 Peter
1:3   150
1:16   260

1 John
4:4   114,217
5:4   262

Detachable Order Form

Please ship_____copies of *No Such Thing As Luck,* for $21.95 each.

Include $2.50 shipping and handling for one book, plus $1.25 for each additional book.

Florida residents must include 7½% sales tax.

Number of books _____ at $21.95 each   Cost $_____

                Plus shipping and handling $_____

         If applicable, 7½% Florida sales tax $_____

                      Total payment $_____

Please charge my ☐Visa   ☐Master card

Name_____

Address_____

City/State/Zip_____

Phone #_____

Credit Card #_____

Exp. Date_____   Signature_____

My check or money order for $_____ is enclosed.

Make your check or money order payable to: **Johnston Publications**

              and send to: **P.O. Box 13**

                     Greenwood, FL 32443

Order by phone: call (850)592-8769

Order by internet: www.johnstonpublications.com

Detachable Order Form

Please ship_____copies of *No Such Thing As Luck,* for $21.95 each.

Include $2.50 shipping and handling for one book, plus $1.25 for each additional book.

Florida residents must include 7½% sales tax.

Number of books _____ at $21.95 each Cost $_____

      Plus shipping and handling $_____

   If applicable, 7½% Florida sales tax $_____

        Total payment $_____

Please charge my ☐Visa ☐Master card

Name_____

Address_____

City/State/Zip_____

Phone #_____

Credit Card #_____

Exp. Date_____ Signature_____

My check or money order for $_____ is enclosed.

Make your check or money order payable to: **Johnston Publications**
and send to: **P.O. Box 13**
Greenwood, FL 32443

Order by phone: call (850)592-8769

Order by internet: www.johnstonpublications.com

Detachable Order Form

Please ship_____copies of *No Such Thing As Luck,* for $21.95 each.

Include $2.50 shipping and handling for one book, plus $1.25 for each additional book.

Florida residents must include 7½% sales tax.

Number of books _____ at $21.95 each   Cost $_____

                             Plus shipping and handling $_____

                  If applicable, 7½% Florida sales tax $_____

                                  Total payment $_____

Please charge my ☐Visa   ☐Master card

Name_____

Address_____

City/State/Zip_____

Phone #_____

Credit Card #_____

Exp. Date_____   Signature_____

My check or money order for $_____ is enclosed.

Make your check or money order payable to: **Johnston Publications**
and send to: **P.O. Box 13**
Greenwood, FL 32443

Order by phone: call (850)592-8769

Order by internet: www.johnstonpublications.com